DELUS

T0317782

HATJE
CANTZ

Issue 0
Autumn 2023

DELUS

The Journal of
the Institute of
Landscape and
Urban Studies

DELUS is an annual publication by the Institute of Landscape and Urban Studies at ETH Zürich. This journal seeks to become a platform for exchange. It brings academic knowledge to a broader audience and fosters dialogue amongst designers, artists, scholars, students and others. Together the themes, topics and methods explored expand the disciplinary boundaries of landscape and urban studies, allowing the journal to embrace a rich dialogue resisting disciplinary silos.

A note from the editors

The Institute of Landscape and Urban Studies (LUS) was launched in 2019 as a collaboration between eight chairs at the Department of Architecture at ETH Zürich; it aims to "address contemporary issues of social equity and environmental transformation." Its research spans the disciplines of "architecture, landscape architecture, urban and regional design, civil engineering, territorial planning and social sciences,"[1] bringing together a constellation of researchers and a variety of topics from the built environment, including but not limited to landscapes, territories and rural and urban areas.

As such, we see the Institute's research ambition as being both expansive (in its purpose and remit) and narrow (in its thematic focus). This somewhat discrepant characteristic begs several key questions: How can the Institute deal with entanglements? Where does one discipline's boundaries end and where does the other discipline's boundaries start? How can critical theory be included in the Institute's research fields? Although each of these questions opens new sets of questions, we see them as pertinent for truly delving into the Institute's *raison d'être*.

Situated at the intersection of architecture, landscape and urban studies, this new journal seeks to become a platform for exchange. It engages with research based at our home institution and far beyond, connecting designers, artists, scientists, scholars and students dealing with landscape and urban questions and giving visibility to emerging topics, concepts and projects in these fields.

For the inaugural issue, we looked beyond our Institute and invited a number of emerging and well-established researchers, practitioners and artists to talk about their approach to research. The inaugural issue took inspiration from a series of lectures held in 2021 in the context of LUS Talks at ETH Zürich, which brought together scholars from different disciplines engaging with landscapes and urban contexts.

Sara Frikech
Johanna Just

1   "Institute of Landscape and Urban Studies," ETH Zürich, lus.arch.ethz.ch.

The talks opened up a wider conversation on new perspectives and research methods that could inspire the field of landscape and urban studies and that are, by necessity, based on cross-disciplinary exchange.

We draw on some of these here, introducing new modes of engagement with tools and artefacts to unpack multiple worlds and narrate diverse stories. The contributions range from unravelling histories of land/body relations through recipes (p. 10), following living fossils and their mythical counterparts (p. 16), working with communities to examine extractive environments (p. 34), exploring postnatural aesthetics (p. 46), to recording acoustic wastelands (p. 56) and developing speculative curricula to favour overlooked forms of action and knowledge (p. 66).

Each contribution in this issue offers a range of diverse insights and directions into landscape and urban questions. As a collection, these contributions address the complex entanglements between humans, non-humans and their environment across time and space. As such, they offer a first glance into the ambitions and approach of this journal that will continuously probe, reflect, experiment, expand, review and revise topics concerning landscape and urban studies. We invite you, our readers, to engage with us and contribute to the discussion regardless of your background. In doing so, this inaugural issue seeks a wide audience and offers a taste of things to come.

As an entry point for this issue, we chose three themes that have been recurring in current discourses, which we have called (Post)-Colonial Temporalities, Plural Ecologies and Digital Futures. Spanning across landscape history, ecology, digital arts and critical humanities, these themes expand the disciplinary boundaries of landscape and urban studies, allowing the journal to embrace a rich dialogue resisting disciplinary silos.

(Post)-Colonial Temporalities underscores how traces of the past are still shaping the present. Existing structures of power rooted in colonial histories continue to exploit both landscapes and bodies. One of the bigger challenges of today is to dismantle and break from the legacies that continue to feed into global inequalities. Scholar and artist Luiza Prado de O. Martins and architectural historian Karin Reisinger describe their respective research journeys in tackling this coloniality of power, showing how it continues to affect both the natural environment and its communities while also foregrounding their collective practices of healing and resistance.

Plural Ecologies probes human/nature relations by acknowledging the shift in paradigm away from the singular narrative rooted in Western tradition and instead pleading to consider the myriad of ways in which humans have engaged with their natural surroundings and continue to do so. It raises the questions of how to include more-than-human actors in our research and how to (un)learn from one another. Urban geographer Sandra Jasper and fresh-water ecologist and artist Christina Gruber give us insights into their findings when dealing with their respective sites of research.

Digital Futures taps into the prospects of digital tools and methods in landscape and urban studies that keep expanding the ways in which we process information and data. It probes into the capacity of new modes of visual representation to capture and translate the complexity of our current planetary condition. The artist Federico Pérez Villoro from the collective Materia Abierta and artists from the Institute for Postnatural Studies suggest speculative curricula and novel aesthetics as ways to engage with the challenges of a changing environment.

Sara Frikech
Johanna Just

More broadly, through this inaugural issue we set off to provide a critical discourse that reflects upon the role of landscape and urban studies within the state of our times. There is no need to spell out the long list of daunting planetary crises and unevenly distributed consequences these entail across generations and geographies. What we highlight here is the importance of reaching out to include a wide range of perspectives, knowledge and experiences, gathering reflective and projective pieces as well as concrete and speculative contributions in an era fraught with enormous challenges.

We would like to thank everyone who supported us in starting DELUS, as well as everyone involved in making this first issue: our contributors, our copy editor, our publisher, as well as our colleagues from the Institute of Landscape and Urban Studies.

Sara & Johanna

DELUS

Salted Waters: Cooking, Land and Resistance

Luiza Prado de O. Martins shows how artefacts of domestic labour allow for unravelling relations of land, body and class within capitalist/colonialist frameworks. She brings us on a journey from biopolitics of coloniality studied through technology to a more personal and profound story exploring how land/body can be understood as part of each other.

Luiza Prado de O. Martins

SETTING THE TABLE

For years, I focused my research on the biopolitics of coloniality; in particular, on how control over fertility was a fundamental trait in the maintenance of colonial structures of power. Defining who gets to have children, how and by what means – these were all key aspects to the maintenance of the organization of labour that sustained colonial economies. Initially, my research led me to investigate technologies like the birth control pill – a medication so important to many, but whose development is inextricably linked to the history of colonization of the Caribbean island of Puerto Rico. During the contraceptive pill's development phase, trials were conducted by US American scientists on patients living in marginalized communities on the island: from the Women's Correctional Institute (a prison in the municipality of Vega Baja) to the public housing development of Rio Piedras (constructed as part of slum clearance efforts). These efforts were partly driven by the perception that poverty was the result of overpopulation: too many mouths to feed and too few resources to attend to that need.

Analyzing the history of the pill and the various structures that made its development possible brought me to examine how colonial relations between the United States and Puerto Rico informed and shaped decisions taken during clinical trials. Principles of informed consent were egregiously transgressed; indeed, lead researchers Gregory Pincus and John Rock dismissed patients' complaints about serious side effects – from depression to thrombosis, to cervical erosion – as results of the "emotional super-activity of Puerto Rican women."[1] They attempted to obscure these issues from prospective trial participants. Similar examples of exploitation of racialized and gendered subjects are unfortunately abundant in the history of birth control and continue to this day.

As I worked through these various historical accounts, I found I could not hold a dispassionate gaze towards these horrifying acts of violence – acts that had been committed within living memory, and that continued to happen to marginalized communities worldwide.

10

1   Annette B. Ramírez de Arellano and Conrad Seipp, *Colonialism, Catholicism, and Contraception: A History of Birth Control in Puerto Rico,* 1st edition (Chapel Hill, NC: The University of North Carolina Press, 2011), 116.

2   Silvia Federici, *Caliban and the Witch: Women, the Body and Primitive Accumulation,* 1st edition (New York, NY: Autonomedia, 2004).

3   Kalpana Wilson, "Population Control, the Cold War and Racialising Reproduction," in *Race, Racism and Development: Interrogating History, Discourse and Practice* (London, New York: Zed Books, 2012), 69–96.

PREVIOUS SPREAD
The Councils of the Pluriversal. Artwork. Luiza Prado de O. Martins, 2019.

How could I have faith in a world where these forms of exploitation keep on happening, over and over again?

SOWING SCARCITY

To answer these questions, a shift in my own approach to the articulations of reproduction and labour was necessary. In uncovering acts of violence, digging deeper into the roots of the biopolitics of coloniality, the broader story of the relationship between land and body comes to life. Marxist feminist scholar Silvia Federici[2] details how land privatization processes initiated in the sixteenth century profoundly impacted gender dynamics, leading to the emergence of a sexual division of labour in Europe that confined women to the domestic realm and fixed them to reproductive work. These processes were underscored by the argument that commoners would be unable to manage the land and food production for the local population would therefore suffer. Land needed, therefore, to be enclosed, put in the hands of the ruling classes who would presumably be able to manage food production. In reality, Federici writes, this form of agrarian capitalism in Europe inaugurated two centuries characterized by waves of starvation among commoners while allowing land owners to profit from the commodification of foodstuffs as goods for export.

The destruction of communal land tenure and stewardship through colonizing processes in Asia, Africa and the Americas had similar effects, triggering processes of land depletion, mass starvation and environmental changes that continue to have dire impacts on these regions today. Examining the context of British-occupied South Asia in the nineteenth century, scholar Kalpana Wilson writes:

[T]he British, in addition to acquiring huge tracts of land for military cantonments for their massively increased military presence, intensified their policy of promoting cash-crop production – particularly wheat and cotton – for export to Britain … the colonial state intervened to redefine the relationship between those who directly cultivated and the land, which became private property. … whereas earlier the main objective was the collection of revenue itself, what was now even more important was that taxation, and the accompanying debt, could be a coercive instrument to ensure the shift from subsistence to cash-crop cultivation.[3]

Wilson brings up a key point here: the privatization of land and the taxation of the working poor were instrumental to guarantee the availability of a class of workers in the colony that would supply the needs of the colonial state. From its early forms, capitalism has required a shift in land/body relations: from land as commons (a foundational requirement for individual and collective well-being) to land as property, commodity and a site of capitalist production. Dispossessed colonial subjects – deprived of access to land and unable to manage and produce food on their own – are thus coerced into performing various forms of waged labour. It is through this process that subjects marginalized because of their race, gender and class become characterized as 'too many' and 'excessive'; scarcity becomes, then, characterized as a function of this excess, rather than a result of dispossession enacted through colonial violence.

Perhaps here the concept of 'distributed reproduction' offers a useful framing to understand the articulations of land, body and class within capitalist/colonialist frameworks. In an article discussing the relationship between biochemical pollutants and settler colonialism, Shadaan and Murphy clarify:

Distributed reproduction names an understanding of reproduction occurring beyond bodies within uneven spatial and temporal infrastructures and relations. This conception of reproduction acknowledges the fulsomeness of Land/body relations, understanding reproduction to exceed the individual body as the site of childbirth and extends into relations to Land. It also attends to the reproductive work of settler infrastructures that distribute the benefits and violences of capitalism and colonialism in particular ways, reproducing and privileging capitalist relations to Land and life.[4]

Articulating the points raised by Shadaan and Murphy with the historical processes described by Federici and Wilson, a rich landscape starts to emerge. The concept of 'overpopulation' has long been weaponized to justify the surveillance of the sexuality and fertility of marginalized peoples, as extensively discussed by authors Dorothy Roberts,[5] Elena Gutiérrez[6] and Angela Davis, among others.

Davis points out that in his 1906 State of the Union address US President Roosevelt "admonished the well born white women who engaged in 'wilful sterility – the one sin for which the penalty is national death, race suicide'."[7] The reproductive labour of white women is framed here as a strategic asset in asserting a settler's right to occupy land, and to the creation and maintenance of a white ethno-state. Concurrently, racialized and gendered subjects are fixed to forms of reproductive labour meant to guarantee the availability of a class of replaceable, exploitable workers – subjects that, although fundamental to its functioning, are excluded from the conception of this white ethno-state and kept in a state of scarcity.

RESISTANCE IS BREWING

Change of scene. I'm watching one of my favourite films, *Leila and the Wolves* (1984).

In it, director Heiny Srour weaves together archival footage and her own storytelling to navigate the complexities of coloniality in Lebanon and Palestine throughout the twentieth century through the eyes and struggles of Arab women. It is a beautiful film, at once impactful, bold and profoundly reverent of its subjects. As it happens with good films, there are a few scenes that will be permanently impressed upon me.

What is, to me, one of the film's most iconic scenes happens right at the beginning. It is the 1920s. Men and boys are in the streets, protesting, chanting "Palestine for the Arabs." As they weave through the streets of the city, a group of British soldiers waits, batons in hand. As the two groups meet, the British soldiers ruthlessly attack the peaceful protestors. The demand for restoration of land sovereignty is met with the only language known by the colonial state: that of violence. A reinforcement arrives: another military regiment – this time armed with guns. The soldiers take position and without missing a beat start shooting at the men and boys while the crowd disperses through narrow streets. Now there are bodies on the ground; those who were able to escape run through a long, narrow street, British soldiers at their heels.

Suddenly, something happens: in the houses and buildings lining the way, women appear behind windows, on balconies and terraces. As the British soldiers pass by, plant pots start raining on their heads, indignation made material. Some members of the colonizing force are hurt; some collapse on the pavement and need to be dragged away. For the first time, the British seem confused, taken by surprise; soldiers run in every direction. A protester runs through an archway into another street; a soldier, close behind, grabs him by the arm. The man shoves him back, but the soldier is armed – it's too late. The shot comes, and the man collapses.

4   Reena Shadaan and Michelle Murphy, "EDC's as Industrial Chemicals and Settler Colonial Structures: Towards a Decolonial Feminist Approach," *Catalyst: Feminism, Theory, Technoscience* 6, no. 1 (2020).

5   Dorothy Roberts, *Killing the Black Body: Race, Reproduction, and the Meaning of Liberty* (New York: Vintage Books, 1998).

6   Elena R. Gutiérrez, *Fertile Matters: The Politics of Mexican-Origin Women's Reproduction* (Austin: University of Texas Press, 2008).

7   Angela Y. Davis, "Racism, Birth Control and Reproductive Rights," in *Feminist Postcolonial Theory: A Reader*, ed. Reina Lewis and Sara Mills, 1st edition (New York: Vintage Books 2003), 353–67.

8   Comité Clandestino Revolucionario Indígena-Comandancia General del Ejército Zapatista de Liberación Nacional, "Cuarta Declaración de la Selva Lacandona 'Enlace Zapatista'," Archivo Histórico, January 1, 1996. enlacezapatista.ezln.org.mx/1996/01/01/cuarta-declaracion-de-la-selva-lacandona.

The film cuts to a scene on a terrace where one woman runs to ask two others: "is the water boiling yet?" They gather around a massive cauldron – the kind used to make a soup or a stew for a family, a community, a group of friends and comrades. Together, the women carry the heavy pot to the edge of the terrace. They drop its contents on the running soldiers beneath. As the boiling water touches their flesh, the men scream, cry, fall to the ground.

I wonder about this cauldron's life story: how many mouths has it been able to feed with a few, simple ingredients? Which fruits, vegetables, herbs, roots or rhizomes (potatoes, onions, carrots, tomatoes, thyme?) have gathered in its rounded metal edges, brought from the river to the sea through the ritual of cooking? Whose hands have stirred (but also grown, foraged and gathered) these precious, life-sustaining ingredients amongst the brutal violence of occupation and land theft? What visions of liberation might have emerged around this cauldron, brought about by the rich, complex scent of spices floating in clouds of steam? What life has been nourished and allowed to flourish through the chaotic generosity of an ever-changing combination of ingredients?

What we see in this scene, however, is a different kind of preparation, a different kind of process. Instead of nourishment, this pot is now meant to cook a weapon. Water – the element of life – transformed through fire in a ritual of resistance and liberation. This too is a form of making community.

The boiling water is poured down from balconies; the attack is disrupted and the soldiers retreat. For a moment, the genocidal impulse of a colonizing force is contained. For a moment, there is celebration, hope, possibility. As the struggle for land unravels, the artefacts of reproductive labour become arms for resistance.

WHAT BELONGS IN THE POT?

The history of a wounded land isn't only made of pain and suffering. It is also a history of soil that gifts, waters that bless and nourish and life that, in spite of hardship, still finds a way to flourish. Rivers that carry away dead leaves, winds that blow in so many directions at once. It is a history of hands working in unison soaking seeds, preparing soil, planting seedlings. Recipes cooked and shared in community; pleasure and care that sustain life. Abundance that defies capitalist scarcity. In their Fourth Declaration from the Lacandona Jungle, the Zapatista Liberation Movement writes:

Many words are walked in the world. Many worlds are made. Many worlds make us. There are words and worlds that are lies and injustices. There are words and worlds that are truthful and true. We make truthful worlds. We are made by truthful words. In the world of the powerful there is space only for the big and their servants. In the world we want there is space for all. The world we want is a world where many worlds fit. The nation we build is one that may fit all the peoples and their languages, that may be walked by all gaits, that may be laughed in, that may be awoken.[8]

In his book *The Poetics of Relation*, poet and philosopher Édouard Glissant proposes the concept of errantry as a material and spatial expression of his concept of Relation. Errantry, in his view, offers both a critique and a complication of rhizomatic thought as proposed by Deleuze and Guattari; whilst the rhizome "maintains … the idea of rootedness but challenges that of a totalitarian root," the nomadism it encompasses can take forms that conceptually sustain colonizing forms of engagement with the world. To illustrate his point, Glissant describes the colonizing process in the Americas as animated by

9 Édouard Glissant, *Poetics of Relation*, trans. Betsy Wing (Ann Arbor: University of Michigan Press, 1997), 18.

the impulse of "arrowlike nomadism" as a practice of land invasion, exploitation and extermination of entire peoples; a manner of engaging with the world that is fundamentally dependent on the separation of a Self from an Other, citizen from foreigner, visitor from visited. Contrastingly, he proposes:

> Errantry … does not proceed from renunciation nor from frustration regarding a supposedly deteriorated (deterritorialized) situation of origin; it is not a resolute act of rejection or an uncontrolled impulse of abandonment … *the thought of errantry is also the thought of what is relative, the thing relayed as well as the thing related.*[9]

What worlds belong in a pot? What are the ingredients of a revolution? What restorative, radical articulations of land/body relations can emerge from the heterogenous chaos of boiling liquids? What secrets can be divined from slowly rising steam? Stews, soups and curries materialize knowledges that migrate, change, shift; dishes meant to nourish families and communities, passed down through generations. In the complexity and shapelessness of rising steam we find a rejection of linear narratives, of the certainty of arrowlike nomadism, of the purity of lineage. In the generosity of a recipe that can always attend to the needs of one more hungry comrade, we find connection and commonality.

These recipes can tell stories, knotted worlds bound by the sacredness of broth; narratives that articulate spaces where ever-evolving forms of caring for one another can emerge across an extended period of time. This type of care work is made of smaller gestures with long-term repercussions, gestures that trouble the narrative of scarcity advanced by capitalism and coloniality and point towards other possibilities, other realities, other worlds where abundance – of time, generosity, affection, patience – is possible. Worlds where land/body are understood to be part of one another; where generative and restorative relationships are possible. In the pot, we find revolution. In salted waters, we find the possibility of life. •

Rivers, Sturgeons and Dragons

Christina Gruber follows sturgeons in the Danube to investigate the evolution of dragon myths along the stream, asking whether the majestic fish can help re-calibrate the relationship between bodies of water and human bodies.

There are two royal fish so styled by the English law writers – the whale and the sturgeon; both royal property under certain limitations, and nominally supplying the tenth branch of the crown's ordinary revenue. I know not that any other author has hinted of the matter; but by inference it seems to me that the sturgeon must be divided in the same way as the whale, the King receiving the highly dense and elastic head peculiar to that fish, which, symbolically regarded, may possibly be humorously grounded upon some presumed congeniality. And thus there seems a reason in all things, even in law.[1]

LEARNING FROM THE RIVER

Over my twelve years of working in, with, on and for rivers, I have learned that precise conclusions are hard to reach. Rivers re-write their history every day, as they are influenced by a multitude of factors. Erosion and accumulation processes shift the appearance of a river regularly and allow pre-historic sands and maybe even gold to re-surface. To study a river means to embrace uncertainty. I learned this for the first time when my colleague Paula Cohen and I travelled down the Danube River to investigate the relationship between river and people.[2] Quickly, it became obvious that this cannot be done without embracing more-than-human bodies. In other words, both the living and non-living entities forming the river network. Throughout our 2000-kilometre-long journey, we talked to many different experts – historians, ecologists, biologists, captains, conservationists, swimmers, outdoor enthusiasts and fishermen. In all these conversations, two species and their story of disappearance appeared repeatedly: the mighty sturgeons and mystical dragons.

In the following visual essay, I focus on the complex life cycle and history of the sturgeon in the Danube as well as on its close relationship to the degradation of complex river ecosystems.[3] Further on, I explore whether sturgeons can help re-establish and re-calibrate our relationship to our bodies of water.[4] Over centuries, sturgeons have played a crucial role for the Danube as cultural

Christina Gruber

16

1 Hermann Melville, *Moby Dick; or The Whale* (London: Richard Bentley, 1851), Chapter 90, 611.

2 The outcome of this was the artists' book: Paula Cohen and Christina Gruber, *From Mud To Outer Space* (Vienna: Soybot, 2017).

3 I am part of the sturgeon conservation project LIFE Sterlet, situated on an artificial island that protects the city of Vienna from floods. The sterlet (*Acipenser ruthenus*) is a small species of sturgeon and the last remaining sturgeon species in the Upper Danube. We aim to strengthen the wild stock of the sterlet sturgeon and to establish healthy and self-sustaining populations in the different sections of the Danube. Every year, we hatch thousands of fish in our hatchery on the Danube Island in Vienna and release juveniles into the river. Even though sturgeons have been around for millions of years, we know little about their habitats. Because of this, we monitor them along the river to make recommendations for their protection and develop a management plan for the sterlet in the Upper Danube.

4 Astrida Neimanis, *Bodies of Water. Posthuman Feminist Phenomenology* (London: Bloomsbury Academic, 2017).

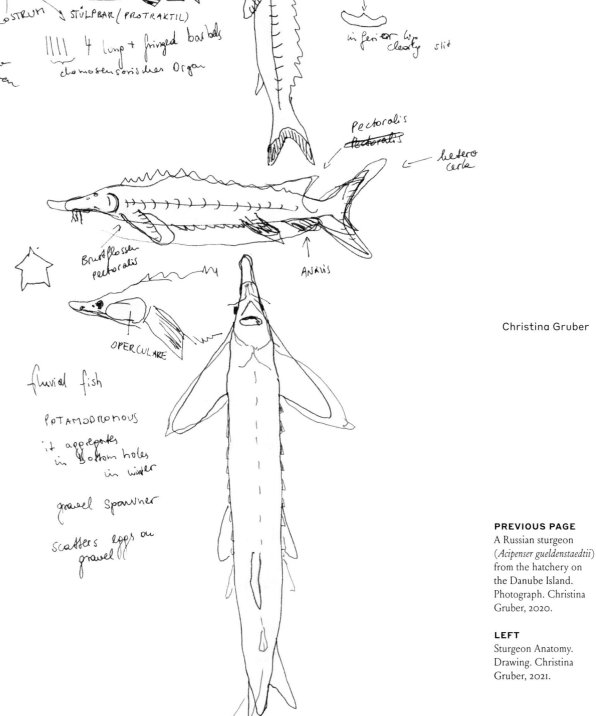

Spritzloch 13 DOR
spines

ROSTRUM STÜLPBAR (PROTRAKTIL)

Elektro
rezeptoren

|||| 4 lang + fringed barbels
chemosensorisches Organ

5 rows of scutes

inferior lip clearly slit

Pectoralis
~~Pectoralis~~

hetero
cerk

Brustflossen
Pectoralis

ANALIS

OPERCULARE

fluvial fish

POTAMODROMOUS

it aggregates
in bottom holes
in winter

gravel spawner

scatters eggs on
gravel

Christina Gruber

PREVIOUS PAGE
A Russian sturgeon
(*Acipenser gueldenstaedtii*)
from the hatchery on
the Danube Island.
Photograph. Christina
Gruber, 2020.

LEFT
Sturgeon Anatomy.
Drawing. Christina
Gruber, 2021.

18

5 Natureculture is a synthesis of nature and culture that recognizes their inseparability in ecological relationships that are both biophysically and socially formed. Donna J. Haraway coined this term in her text *The Companion Species Manifesto: Dogs, People, and Significant Otherness*, Vol. 1 (Chicago: Prickly Paradigm Press, 2003).

6 Fengzhi He, Christiane Zarfl, Vanessa Bremerich, Alex Henshaw, William Darwall, Klement Tockner and Sonja C. Jaehnig, "Disappearing Giants: A Review of Threats to Freshwater Megafauna," in: *Wiley Interdisciplinary Reviews*: Water 4, no. 3 (2017).

7 Thomas Friedrich, "Biodiversity Conservation: the Role of Large Flagship Fish Species and Small Endemites," (PhD dissertation, University of Natural Resources and Life Sciences in Vienna, 2020).

8 Ivan Jarić, Jörn Gessner and Mirjana Lenhardt, "A life-table metamodel to support the management of data deficient species, exemplified in sturgeons and shads," *Environmental Biology of Fishes* 98 (2015): 2337–52.

9 Thomas Friedrich, Jörn Gessner, Ralf Reinartz and Beate Striebel, "Pan-European Action Plan for Sturgeons," adopted by the Standing Committee of the Convention on the Conservation of European Wildlife and Natural Habitats (Bern Convention) in the 38th

heritage, as an important food source and as a key indicator of a healthy aquatic ecosystem; as such, sturgeon sightings were often related to myths and folk stories and shaped her *natureculture* relationship.[5] If we let these last dragons disappear, we will lose a significant part of the Danube's identity forever.

MUDDY REFLECTIONS OF THE PAST

Sturgeons (*Acipenseridae*) are part of the freshwater megafauna in temperate regions of North America and Eurasia. Archaeological findings trace them back to over 200 million years when they started to inhabit the earth's water bodies; sturgeons have remained almost unchanged since then. These living fossils can grow up to seven meters long and weigh up to 1.5 tons. Bony scutes – like dragons – overlay their bodies and protect them from predators. Their bodies mark a transition within the group of bony fishes, because they are formed by cartilage; this can be seen as an embodied transition. Both their appearance and life-span seem to be positioned outside of time, as they can live to be up to 200 years old. They reflect the waters they inhabit – muddy, blurry and gigantic.

Throughout time, they have been the subject of many great stories, preventing people from sleeping at night and haunting their dreams. Even today their life cycle cannot be completely demystified by scientists.

Due to their prehistoric look, size, longevity and life cycle, sturgeons are of high interest to different groups including conservationists, mythologists, scientists, literature scholars and entrepreneurs. Still, we have lost touch with these prehistoric beings, as they inhabit large muddy waters and are hard to follow. Research on Danube sturgeons is structurally underfunded and as such, sturgeon population monitoring is poor. Unless something changes, this will lead to the silent and unnoticed loss of the last large flagship species of the Danube.[6]

Sturgeon species' names are reminiscent of their shape and sound heroic: beluga (*Huso huso*), Russian sturgeon (*Acipenser gueldenstaedtii*), ship sturgeon (*A. nudiventris*) and stellate sturgeon (*A. stellatus*). Only one species – like a lone knight of the King's guard – can still be found in very small, isolated populations in the Upper Danube: the sterlet (*A. ruthenus*), the smallest of the five Danube sturgeons. The ship sturgeon is possibly extinct in the Black Sea and Danube. Russian sturgeon, beluga and stellate sturgeon are critically endangered and restricted to the Lower Danube.[7]

BLACK GOLD AND OBSTACLES

Overfishing and the disruption of the river continuum in the last century have led to the extinction of large anadromous sturgeon species in the Middle and Upper Danube. Considering sturgeons' bony armour and tragic fate, we could truly describe humans as having become 'dragon slayers.'

The precious sturgeon eggs are highly valued goods and one of the reasons they are facing extinction. For centuries, sturgeons were an important food source as their large bodies could provide for entire families. To this day, their eggs (caviar) are one of the most expensive delicacies. Sturgeons can take up to twenty years to mature; if they are caught before their first reproduction, an entire generation is at stake.[8] This calls for strict regulations on the fishing of wild sturgeons and for close monitoring and active implementation of these regulations.[9]

Besides being a desired food source, sturgeons have been thought of as dragons of the river. Even nowadays, buildings, plates, emblems and furniture carvings display their shape. Instead of fire, their bellies store a weapon – a kind of black gold.

The first records of overfishing trace back to the Middle Ages. The most drastic decline of the sturgeon population happened in the last century with the installation of migration barriers.

Christina Gruber

LEFT
Pre-historic view of the
Austrian Danube region
resembling a swamp
landscape. Collage.
Christina Gruber, 2017.

Meeting, November 30, 2018.

10 Ian J. Harrison and Melanie L. J. Stiassny, "The Quiet Crisis. A Preliminary Listing of the Freshwater Fishes of the World that are Extinct or Missing in Action," in *Extinctions in Near Time*, eds. Ross D. E. MacPhee and Hans-Dieter Sues (New York: Kluwer Academic/Plenum Publishers, 1999), 271–331.

11 He *et al.*, "Disappearing Giants" (see note 6).

12 Severin Hohensinner, Christoph Hauer and Susanne Muhar, "River Morphology, Channelization, and Habitat Restoration," in *Riverine Ecosystem Management—Science for Governing Towards a Sustainable Future*, eds. Stefan Schmutz and Jan Sendzimir (Cham, Switzerland: Springer, 2018), 41–65.

13 Osvaldo E. Sala, F. I. I. I. Stuart Chapin, Juan J. Armesto, Eric Berlow, Janine Bloomfield, Rodolfo Dirzo, Elisabeth Huber-Sanwald *et al.* "Global Biodiversity Scenarios for the Year 2100," *Science* 287, no. 5459 (2000): 1770–74.

Sturgeons travel long distances (from the sea up the river) to find their spawning grounds, which are often close to their own birthplace. This behaviour is referred to as *homing*. Currently, these migratory routes are blocked by barriers such as hydropower plants and dams.[10]

In fact, the biggest decline in sturgeon numbers can be traced back to the installation of big hydropower dams along the Danube to produce energy that occurred in the last century.[11] After World War II, many dams were installed in the Upper Danube; in the Middle and Lower Danube, only two dams prevent sturgeons from their migration. The biggest of these dams are the Iron Gate Dams (I and II) located between Romania and Serbia. Their construction finished in 1972 and changed the environment for the sturgeons forever, impeding their migration after some hundred kilometres (rather than after 2000 kilometres, as before). This migratory barrier prevented sturgeons' instinctive urge to migrate back to their birthplace to lay their eggs, i.e. bringing an end to *homing*. It also marked the end of the island Ada Kaleh, a Turkish enclave in the middle of the Danube. This island had become famous as hotspot of biodiversity – a gathering place for a wide assortment of species, but also for writers, political refugees and other historical figures. The dam turned the most powerful beings of the river into an endangered species.

The continuous regulation and straightening of the Danube represented another impediment to the sturgeon population as it led to the loss of their important habitats. One hundred and fifty years ago, the channelization of the Danube started with the creation of a steady navigation line. The riverbed was dug out and its shorelines were reinforced. This meant the decoupling of floodplains and the degradation of important wetlands.[12]

Already back then, local fishermen warned that the decoupling of the vast floodplain systems and the creation of one steady main course would lead to the degradation of the river and the loss of many fish species that are dependent on different aquatic habitats throughout the year and during their lifetime. The Global Freshwater Fish Assessment conducted by the International Union for Conservation of Nature (IUCN) states that 75% of global wetlands were lost during the twentieth century and that freshwater fish populations declined by 83% between 1970 and 2014.[13]

Biodiversity, complexity and the unexpected twists and turns of the river were replaced with uniformity and predictability to suit the needs of the dragon slayers. Throughout this drastic change, myth and sagas lived on. These narratives are part of the Danuban identity and shape the cultural and natural heritage of this region. Still, most of these stories seem to disappear quicker than ever. Therefore, it is time to preserve them and add new ones to underline the importance of sturgeons for healthy rivers and hence people living along them.

STURGEONS AS ENVIRONMENTAL SENSORS

Heritage is based on common memory and the selection of spoken words makes it into books. Many things get lost in translation, but trying to manifest the experiences can be the beginning of new stories and fictions. Finding the sturgeon on a menu in a restaurant in Gemenc (HU) makes me wonder about all the things lost and found again. Maybe they just need to be re-ignited, like an open fire, so commonly used for barbecues in the Balkans. •

STERLET
Acipenser ruthenus

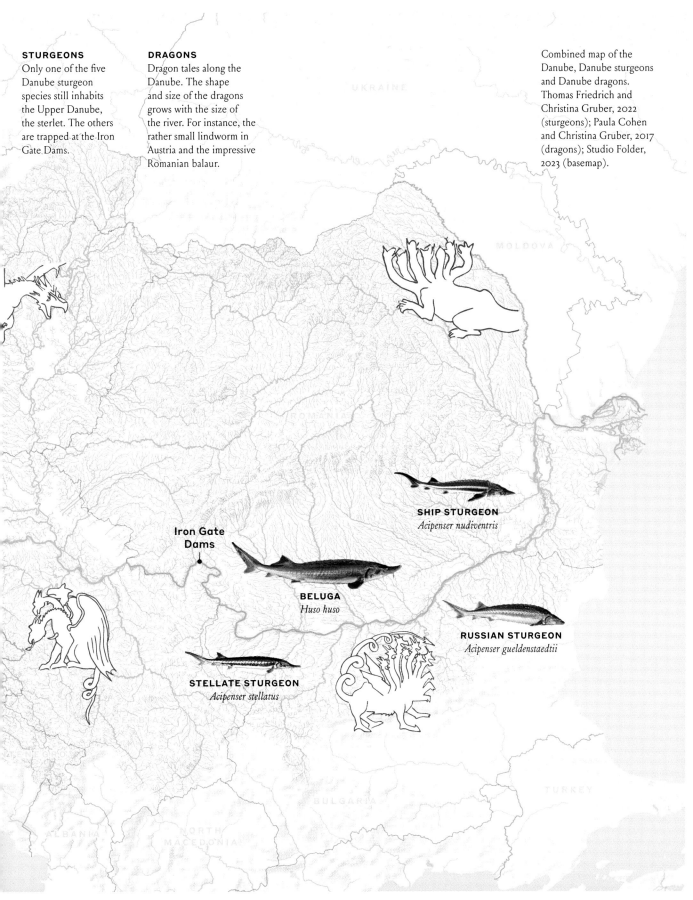

STURGEONS
Only one of the five Danube sturgeon species still inhabits the Upper Danube, the sterlet. The others are trapped at the Iron Gate Dams.

DRAGONS
Dragon tales along the Danube. The shape and size of the dragons grows with the size of the river. For instance, the rather small lindworm in Austria and the impressive Romanian balaur.

Combined map of the Danube, Danube sturgeons and Danube dragons. Thomas Friedrich and Christina Gruber, 2022 (sturgeons); Paula Cohen and Christina Gruber, 2017 (dragons); Studio Folder, 2023 (basemap).

Iron Gate Dams

SHIP STURGEON
Acipenser nudiventris

BELUGA
Huso huso

RUSSIAN STURGEON
Acipenser gueldenstaedtii

STELLATE STURGEON
Acipenser stellatus

Christina Gruber

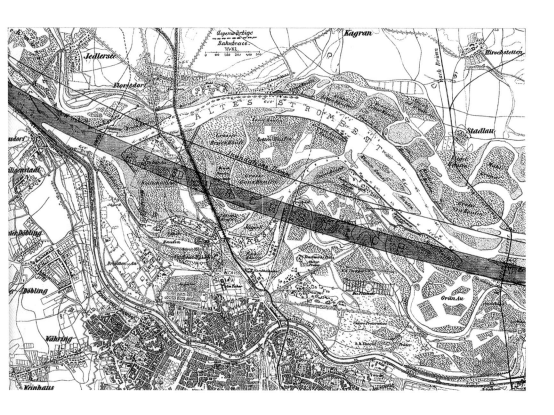

A A view onto the submerged Ada Kaleh island. Photograph. Christina Gruber, 2017.

B Plans for channel-ization of the Danube in Vienna by the Danube Regulation Commission between 1870 and 1875. In: Raimund Hinkel, *Wien XXI. Floridsdorf. Das Heimatbuch.* Vienna, 1994.

C-D Muddy Reflections of the Danube. Photograph. Christina Gruber, 2017.

E Kilometer Zero. Where the river meets the sea. Photograph. Christina Gruber, 2017.

F Danube Delta. Photograph. Christina Gruber, 2017.

G   Hydropower
Plant Aschach, Austria.
Photograph.
FOTO:FORTEPAN/
Drobni Nándor, 1964,
(CC BY-SA 3.0).

H   Fishermen of the
Volga River, Russia, with
their impressive catch
of beluga sturgeons.
Unknown source, 1924.
Retrieved from: imgur.
com/gallery/nuSzb.

I   Beluga (*Huso huso*).
Photograph. Thomas
Friedrich, 2018.

J   Beluga catch in
the Wallachian lowlands
using sturgeon fences.
Etching by Jakob Alt.
In: Alt and Ermini
(1824), Institute of
Hydrobiology and
Water Management
BOKU Vienna, 2014.

Christina Gruber

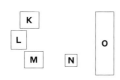

K Sfanthu Georghe, painting of George killing a dragon in the Lipovan village, Slava Cercheza in the Danube Delta. Photograph. Christina Gruber, 2017.

L *Das Buch von Kaiser Sigismund*, folio 89r, King Sigismund and a number of German princes in a large boat, fishing for sturgeon in the River Waag, as two large fish lurk underneath the boat's keel. Eberhard Windeck, ca. 1440–50.

M Sturgeon fresco, Italian church in the Po region. Photograph. Thomas Wolkinger, 2021.

N Meso-/Neolithic stone sturgeon sculpture from Lepenski Vir at the Iron Gates, around 6 700–8 500 years old. Photograph. Christina Gruber, 2017.

O *Eve and the Dragon*, Cathédrale Notre-Dame, Reims. Photograph. Vassil, 2007.

Christina Gruber

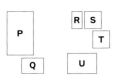

P-Q Monitoring, artificial reproduction, tagging, acoustic telemetry, release of juvenile sturgeons into the Danube. Photograph. LIFE Sterlet, 2021.

R-U Sturgeon reproduction, larvae in their hatching jars, sturgeon conservation of a white sturgeon from a pond. Photograph. Christina Gruber, 2021.

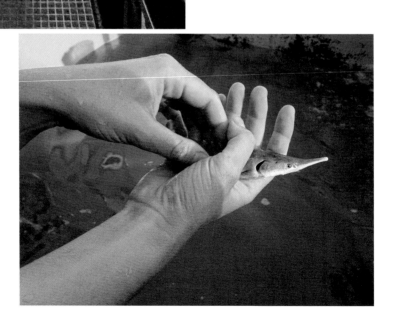

Christina Gruber

V LIFE Sterlet
hatchery container on
the Danube Island in
Vienna. Photograph.
Christina Gruber, 2019.

W Juvenile sterlet
in the hands of the
caretaker. Photograph.
Christina Gruber, 2020.

X The bony scutes of
Acipenser gueldenstaedtii,
one of the five remaining
Danube sturgeons.
Photograph. Thomas
Friedrich, 2018.

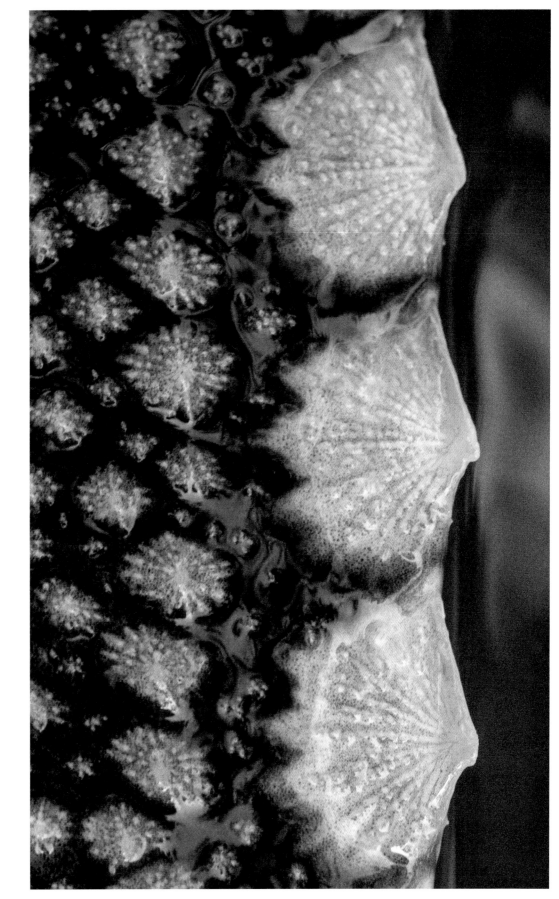

Feminist Responses to the Prolonged Colonialities of Exploited Landscapes

In conversation with Karin Reisinger, we reflect on historical research methods combined with participatory formats. She brings out marginalized voices and material relations and examines the prolonged coloniality of exploited mining landscapes in the peripheries of northern Sweden.

JOHANNA JUST Your work aims to complexify the narratives of exploited landscapes of northern Sweden in order to uncover the prolonged coloniality of these places. Could you briefly provide some context of your ongoing research and how you started working on these topics?

Interview with
Karin Reisinger

KARIN REISINGER Within the mining landscapes of northern Sweden, the predominant narratives in historiography but also on a day-to-day basis are heroic and predominantly male – demonstrating dominant cultures and dominant ways of dealing with nature. As a result, complexifying the narratives is an important task for knowledge production. For instance, this area of the country is generally known for and depicted by the hard labour of the mining and the technological advancements or sophistication and experimentation of architectures in remote places – although these go hand in hand with the exploitation of the country. In this context, it seemed necessary to me to give voice to the people who are losing their homes and their living environments due to the extraction of minerals. It is important to look closely at how exploitation takes place and what the effects are for various humans and non-humans.

My interest in following the concrete material connections of the profession of architecture (building materials) and the extractive areas (resources) was awakened by the exhibition 'Dokumentera Malmberget' at the sports hall of Malmberget. In 2016, I visited the towns of Kiruna, Malmberget and Gällivare for the first time. In these towns, the state-owned Swedish mining company LKAB extracts iron ore on a daily basis; the amount which is extracted is equivalent to building eleven Eiffel towers a day. At the time, it had already become clear that Malmberget

1 See samelandsfriauniversitet.com/blogg/archives/02-2017.

2 May-Britt Öhman organized a panel with the speakers Henrik Andersson, Tor Lundberg Tuorda and Gunilla Larsson at "Undisciplined Environments," International Conference of the European Network of Political Ecology (ENTITLE) co-organized by Environmental Humanities Laboratory of the Division of History of Science, Technology and Environment at KTH Royal Institute of Technology, Stockholm and the Center for Social Studies of the University of Coimbra, March 20–24, 2016. ces.uc.pt/undisciplined-environments/docs/UndEnv_final_programme.pdf.

3 See also Karin Reisinger, "Doing Material Positionality while Listening to the Prolonged Coloniality of a Mining Town on Indigenous Ground," in *Architectures of Colonialism: Constructed Histories, Conflicting Memories*, ed. Vera Egbers, Christa Kamleithner, Özge Sezer, Alexandra Skedzuhn-Safir and Albrecht Wiesener (Basel: Birkhäuser, forthcoming).

4 Erik Simander, "Ny rättslig runda för Kallak-projektet," [New legal round for the Kallak project] *Dagens Nyheter*, June 20, 2022. dn.se/sverige/ny-rattslig-runda-for-kallak-projektet/.

5 To mention just a few: see for example Astrid Andersen, Kirsten Hvenegård-Lassen and Ina Knobblock, "Feminism in Postcolonial Nordic Spaces," NORA – *Nordic*

would not exist in the future due to the ground becoming unstable as a result of the advancement of the underground mining (FIG. B). The town is therefore divided by a huge pit called the Captain's Pit. In the adjacent sports hall, a large exhibition was organized by the town's inhabitants to display its past with a huge model and a large number of photographs. I was greatly impressed with how local knowledge and skills were used for urgently preserving heritage, without waiting for the professionalized and institutionalized expertise of heritage. Nevertheless, I missed the perspectives of women and of the Indigenous population of the area, the Sámi. Women's perspectives were displayed in a separate room upstairs, but the Indigenous voices were not visible. This was one of the key motivations for staying with these issues. I started looking for broader perspectives and the polyphonic voices of the Anthropocene.

SARA FRIKECH   Can you elaborate a bit on the Indigenous voices?

KR   Sápmi, the Indigenous land of the Sámi, covers a vast area in Norway, Sweden, Finland and Russia. This is not well known in Central Europe, although Indigeneity is now much discussed in the art discourse. There are discussions on Indigeneity and colonialism, but Sámi voices are still not present enough.

When I was a postdoc fellow at KTH Stockholm, I started working with Sweden's mining territories to understand the material entanglements of the profession of architecture – the material entanglements with naturecultures that are far away from our exploitative lifestyles but materially (and economically) connected. Shortly after I arrived in Stockholm in 2016, a remarkable workshop organized by May-Britt Öhman from the Sámi Land Free University[1] informed the audience about local effects of the exploitation of the north for the Sámis.[2] For centuries, the rights and possibilities of Indigenous people to use their land have been limited as a result of resources being quarried in the north of Sweden.[3] The situation is still conflictual and even more difficult due to the massive interventions linked to the production of energy and the overall situation of climate change. Recently, the Swedish state gave permission to a British mining company to exploit resources in a new mine in Gallók on Indigenous land near Jokkmokk.[4]

Researchers with connections to Indigeneity have been looking at the intersection of Swedish colonialism and gender. Awareness is growing about how the colonization of the north of the country also imported concepts of gender.[5] For me, it was important to follow connections between architecture and material exploitation (which results in the exploitation of various bodies) to this complex history of effects, agencies and struggles. Building materials such as steel come from places like the area of Malmberget. I wanted to see how this material extraction plays out for the various actors living there.

sf   As a researcher, you observe and engage with situated knowledges and practices stemming from what you call 'feminist ecologies' and their 'productive spaces' in soon to be post-extractive[6] living environments. Can you elaborate on the notion of 'feminist ecologies' in the mining areas you study? What can we learn from this notion?

kr   By 'feminist-ecologist,' I mean discussions from the last one to two decades around feminist political ecologies, feminist new materialisms/critical materialisms and feminist posthumanisms. That's what I refer to when I roughly summarize these discussions as feminist ecologies. Yet I think it's also a very productive term because it demands that all ecological changes need to be addressed with feminist questions. Who owns the material? Who profits from it? Who is being exploited? The fields of feminist new materialisms, posthumanisms and political ecologies have created an interesting discourse around these questions and complexified them. This discourse is well capable of taking on an intersectional approach, including race, ethnicity, ableism and class and so on.[7] Discussions of feminist political ecologies, for example, are always connected to the situated knowledges, local effects and knowledge that results from these.

Local feminist practitioners respond to extraction activities, sometimes on small scales but in large numbers and varieties. For example, the embroidery cafe was founded by Karina Jarrett in Gällivare, the neighbouring town of the disappearing town of Malmberget. In this group, women come together to embroider. They also embroider the houses that are going to be lost because of the advancement of mining. There are many practices taking place locally. Pernilla Fagerlönn curated and organized a farewell festival for the last high-rise building of Malmberget, the 'Farväl Focus.' Through this cultural festival involving local artists, the inhabitants of Malmberget could bid farewell to the last remaining thirteen-storey building before it was taken down. The local artist Miriam Vikman painted the façades of the houses before they were dismantled. The collaboration with these actors is very relevant for my work, and also creates connections between the actors. The next step is to bring them together. I'm also working with the Austrian mining town of Eisenerz (literally 'iron ore') at the foot of Erzberg ('ore mountain'). Building up these types of networks of cultural exchange (i.e. between actors in Sweden and Austria) through shared practices will enable these actors to come into conversation, which is of course something they already do; but what I want to do is also weave these conversations into a slowly growing net of various forms of cooperation between research and local practices (FIG. D, E).[8]

JJ   Our next question builds upon this idea of your own positionality as a researcher and on subjectivity. Working and seeing with communities in precarious contexts requires a form of care and awareness.

Journal of Feminist and Gender Research 23, no. 4 (2015): 239–45; Madina Tlostanova, Suruchi Thapar-Björkert and Ina Knobblock, "Do We Need Decolonial Feminism in Sweden?" *NORA – Nordic Journal of Feminist and Gender Research* 27, no. 4 (2019): 290–95. See also Emma Göransson, *Postnomadiska landskap* (Stockholm: Arkitektur- och designcentrum, 2017); Ina Knobblock, *Writing-Weaving Sámi Feminisms: Stories and Conversation* (Lund: Lund University, 2022).

6 The term 'post-extractive' as it is used here means concerning the time after the extraction, when resources will have expired.

7 Sarah E. Truman has claimed from feminist new materialisms a "feminism that attends to race, gender, sexuality, and ability." Sarah E. Truman, "Feminist New Materialisms" in *The SAGE Encyclopedia of Research Methods*, eds. Paul A. Atkinson, Sara Delamont, M. A. Hardy and M. Williams (London, UK: SAGE Publications, 2019).

8 This research is funded by the Austrian Science Fund (FWF), project no. TI157-G.

9 Jane Rendell, "Giving an Account of Oneself: Architecturally," *Journal of Visual Culture* 15, no. 3 (2016): 334–48.

How have you questioned your own positionality as a researcher? Do you include your own subjectivity during your field research? And how has this shaped your research, the relationships you have with the people on site and how you work with them?

KR   To me, the question of positionality is linked to communication and to how we come together in these exploited landscapes. It means introducing (and thus positioning) ourselves[9] to make clear where we (the researchers) are coming from, what informs our questions, how these become relevant and what the answers of the questions might lead to. I (personally, and as an architect) am connected to these extractive landscapes via material. For example, the conversation we're having right now is also facilitated by material; we are streaming this with the computer and to do this we are dependent on mineral resources. Without these materials, we could not work or communicate at all. Especially as architects, we are dependent on what is being produced in Malmberget or in other mines in north Sweden. These mines are by far the strongest providers of iron ore Europe-wide. But the global supply chain of iron ore was reshuffled in 2022 as a result of the political situation that led to looking for resources within Europe to avoid politically problematic dependencies. These types of reshufflings bring to the fore a series of entanglements. Take for example steel, which we use a lot of in building in architecture. Understanding these entanglements is why I also want to dare to think about how we are always already entangled in these environments. That is the position I come from. And that's how I start the conversation. On the ground, when I begin research, it is important to be able to explain to people why I am there, and what I do there. What is my concern? How am I concerned? And I think it is a very good starting point to begin with a material positionality by explaining that we are all in this process of material exchange – but in different ways.

SF   What does the process look like when you work with the communities? Does it take you a lot of time to build trust?

KR   For me it is a very slow process. Also, the disappearance of the community of Malmberget is a very slow process (**FIG. C**). It was clear already in the 1950s that this community would not exist in the future; this became official in the 1970s. The dismantling of the community is extremely slow and my process of building all these connections with the community is likewise very slow. I had more than fifteen stays in the area. My engagement is slow to follow the changes over the years. There is a lot of back and forth and it is very important to look at the ethics of this exchange because there is knowledge extractivism just as there is material extractivism. I always try to give something back. The material positionality, as I would call it, is the start of a conversation;

but also the continuous collaborations that lead to shared authorships[10] often mean adhering to the tempi, languages and needs of local actors.

JJ   Following up on the materiality that you're talking about and the connectivity through materials: Do you think the type of material you are researching plays a role? And in what terms does the iron ore, which is often perceived as a masculine material, influence how you approach the research?

KR   That is an interesting question. I am sure it does. I started working with the community, the local practices and the landscape before I looked at this material connection. But I'm sure that iron ore, in particular, comes with male-dominated narratives. The images found in various iron ore mining towns are quite telling of these narratives. There are lots of historical images of men doing hard work in the mines, despite the fact that there have always been women involved in various stages. And then there is also this heroic narrative of what you can do with iron ore, the agency of the material, but also some kind of conditionality. For example, iron ore is needed for medical products – so there is some kind of unavoidability of exploitation implied. It is necessary to extract large masses to get to the ore-rich minerals. And even these are only partly iron ore. Hence, there are tons of materials extracted, and only a percentage of these are actually usable. Vast masses have to be dumped somewhere else. This has challenged me even more to look at the effects of these movements for a broad variety of local actors.

SF   What can researchers in extended fields of architectural humanities offer these areas in crisis? And how can architectural research foreground perspectives that are often overlooked?

KR   That's a tricky question. I will start with a small example. Basically, I am trying to give back to the communities and also serve them. Of course, I do not want to be too romantic about it but there are moments when things suddenly come together and make sense. For example, in 2019, I gave a participatory lecture in Gällivare, bringing the knowledge of the architectural archive to the community and sharing information about the architectures that are just about to disappear (**FIG. D**). Magazines of the collections of the Architecture and Design Center in Stockholm, the Swedish capital contained donated folders of drawings that nobody had opened before. Nobody was working with the material at all. And the people who are living in these houses have never seen this material. They were, of course, curious about it. I offered to give a lecture at the library. The librarian said: "Of course, if you like, you can do it. But maybe only five people will come." Instead, it was about eighty people coming from this very small town.

10 See for example Karina Jarrett and Karin Reisinger, "Broderi som respons på förlust och sorg," [Embroidery as Response to Loss and Mourning], *Täcklebo Broderiakademi* 2–4 (2021): 26–29; Karin Reisinger and Karina Jarrett, "Karina Jarrett on the Embroidery Café," Video, Repository of the Academy of Fine Arts Vienna, 2021. repository.akbild.ac.at/de/alle_inhalte/; Pernilla Fagerlönn, Ulli Gollesch and Karin Reisinger, "Extraction and Care: Curating Ore Mountains," discussion at Rostfest, Zentrum Münichtal, August 19, 2022. rostfest.at/artists/extraction-and-care-curating-ore-mountains.

It was fantastic to have this conversation – although difficult with such a large group. Afterwards, a woman approached me and said that it was really good that an expert from the outside – that was how my role was perceived although I tried to avoid this – could confirm that high-quality architecture is being lost through the exploitation of the whole landscape. The woman said that this contributed to the local process of mourning the environment they are losing.

I tried to be flexible with these kinds of interventions on the local ground. Also, on the side of knowledge production within academia I added collages to the original drawings, which are still accessible in the archive (**FIG. F, G**). We can look at architectures from the drawings from the 1930s or 1950s – following the great projections created by the capital, planning for this landscape 1 000 kilometres away. We can also look at these architectures at exactly the moment they are being dismantled. I added this layer to the archives, unveiling the details that were in the drawings, in order to expose the architectural details as they became visible during the dismantlement of the buildings. I also want to make this kind of knowledge productive for researchers and work against the binaries of periphery and centre, where knowledge is extracted and where knowledge is stored.

SF　When you do your readings of the architectural sources – trying to deconstruct what is going on with the plans and other architectural material – do interesting findings emerge from your specific way of looking at the projects, knowing the places from your visits and building on your interest in feminist ecologies and productive spaces?

KR　The residential buildings and the planning of the residential buildings from the 50s for example pretty much reveal concepts of gender that are applied with mining. I wondered why the managers' villas are so large, but they were just planned for huge families. A family concept was inscribed in these architectures, commissioned by the mining company. For example, residential buildings for young men called *Ungkarlsbostäder* were planned to attract young single men to come to a town above the polar circle to work in the mines (**FIG. H**). Concepts of gender can also be found in the details. I was looking, for example, at the drawings in the archive from the 50s in Malmberget, mostly by the architect Folke Hederus. Photos by Sune Sundahl, the very prominent Swedish architecture photographer, and Lennart Nilsson (**FIG. A**), a very influential Swedish photographer, complement these drawings. Mostly men were being represented in the architectural photos and in the drawings from Malmberget. I found only one drawing of a woman in the archive (**FIG. F**). It is a very interesting drawing. We can see her pushing a baby stroller. You can only see her back and she is walking through a row of houses that look actually quite unspectacular but have really interesting and innovative sections. Despite the fantastic typologies, the way the woman with the stroller is represented in this drawing, turning her face away from the spectator (slightly behind trees that are actually at the centre of the image), is quite symptomatic of gender roles being imported with respective architectures commissioned by the mining company. It is very interesting to see how representation in the architectural drawings shows these gender concepts.

As always, more examples could be mentioned here. However, the important point is that following the material makes it possible to look at feminism and colonialism at the same time – important, but challenging and not always conflict-free. •

Interview with
Karin Resisinger

B

A   **C**

A Area of Malmberget.
Photograph. Lennart
Nilsson, 1950
(approximate date).
© Lennart Nilsson,
LKAB, Gällivare
Bildarkiv.

B The landscape of
Malmberget in 2022.
Photograph. Karin
Reisinger, 2022.

C Dismantling archi-
tectures of Malmberget
in 2022. Photograph.
Karin Reisinger, 2022.

Interview with
Karin Resisinger

D Participatory lecture in Gällivare Folkets Hus in 2019. Photograph. Ann Maudsley, 2019.

E Karin Reisinger, installation in the ArkDes archives 2018, part of the symposium 'Architectural History at ArkDes' organized by Christina Pech and Mikael Andersson. December 18, 2018. Photograph. Karin Reisinger, 2018.

F *Lifelike Appendix to the Archive No. 1,* 2018–19, Karin Reisinger. Drawing. Architect Folke Hederus, 1957, commissioned by LKAB. Accessible at ArkDes Collections. Photograph. ArkDes/ Björn Strömfeldt.

G *Lifelike Appendix
to the Archive No. 1,*
2018–19, Karin
Reisinger. Drawing.
Architect Folke
Hederus, 1958,
commissioned by
LKAB. Accessible at
ArkDes Collections.
Photograph. ArkDes/
Björn Strömfeldt.

H *Ungkarlsbostäder*
[flats for young men].
Drawing. Architect
Folke Hederus,
1957. Accessible at
ArkDes Collections.
Photograph. ArkDes/
Björn Strömfeldt.

Melting Ecologies

The Institute for Postnatural Studies employs storytelling and artistic research methods to challenge the aesthetic qualities of a melting world – taking as a starting point the concept of *postnature* as a framework for creation.

The Institute for Postnatural Studies is a centre for artistic experimentation from which to explore and problematize postnature as a framework for contemporary creation. Conceived as a platform for critical thinking, it is a network that brings together artists and researchers concerned about the issues of the global ecological crisis through experimental formats of exchange and production of open knowledge. In doing so, the Institute develops long-term research focused on issues such as ecology, coexistence, politics and territories. In the context of the ecological debate, these texts rethink, from our multidisciplinary approach, the mobilizations of matter and their relation to the technological and infrastructural. Based on the vocabulary and deep time of the geology that encompasses and precedes them, they revolve around the perpetual stratifications and de-stratifications (human, non-human, more-than-human) of matter.

Melting Ecologies deal with contemporary aesthetics related to the climate crisis, reflecting on how the technologies that have mediated the world – the representations of nature that have shaped the imaginaries of what natural means – are facing new material but also economic and political complexities. Through these computer-distorted images of postnatural territories, landscapes and materialities, a new dark aesthetic merges jpgs, data and information, proposing an experimental approach to how this melting world is being rendered.

It is obvious that the technologies of representation of nature have always mediated our shared image of what a forest, sunset or landscape mean. Each culture, and each moment, has represented nature from its specific perspective, turning it into one of the most complex cultural constructs of modernity. In our effort to de-romanticize the image of nature, we detach its representations from beauty. A new ecology of images has to include the new materialities and viscous hyperobjects that cover the Earth's crust, but also its invisible layers – rendered tangible through technologies of visualization such as images, softwares, charts ... Such new mediations become transcendental and allow us to understand the complexities and layers that merge while thinking and visualizing the climate crisis.

Institute for
Postnatural Studies

46

Melting Ecologies mostly refer to the invisible.

ALL IMAGES
Melting Ecologies. Artwork. Institute for Postnatural Studies/Matteo Guarnaccia, 2022.

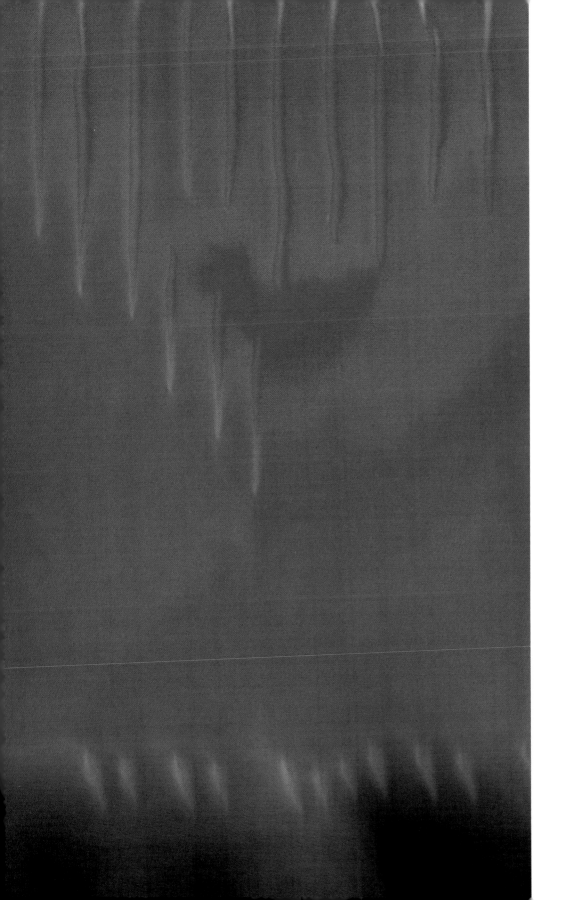

The world is melting, not only in a physical way but also in an exponential way – augmenting its temperature due to the huge amount of energy and heat released into the atmosphere by machines and technologies.

The world is also melting conceptually, ontologically. As such, the categories in which modernity tries to organize and categorize reality are mixing, blurring – just as air particles mix together.

To de-romanticize the image of nature, we need to detach its representations from beauty. An image of contemporary ecology should include its problems, contradictions and infinite layers.

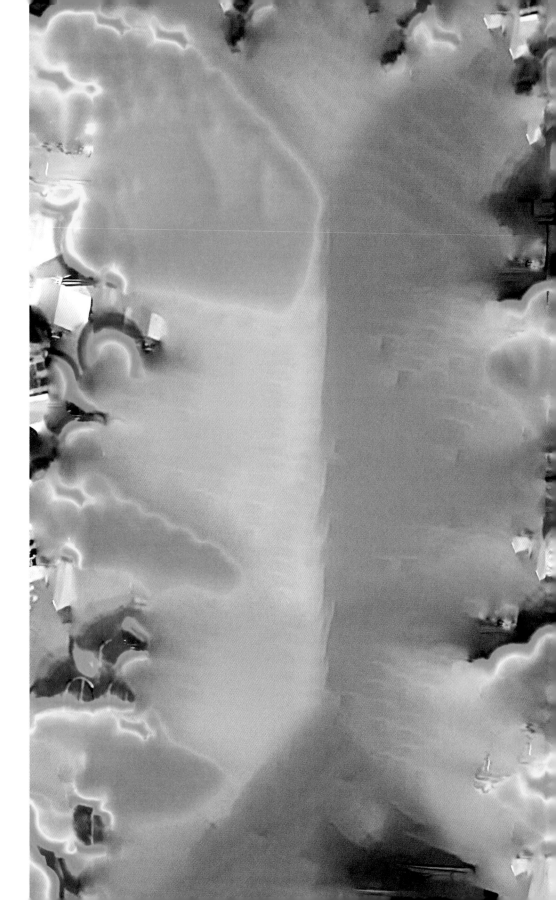

Melting Ecologies
show how technology
and geology merge
to form postnatural
matter that defies cate-
gorizations and blurs
the limits between
culture and nature
and between human
and non-human. Such
testimonies of the
Anthropocene turn
materiality into a political, technological and
economic amalgam.

New melting materi-
alities become instant
archaeological ruins
of a new era.

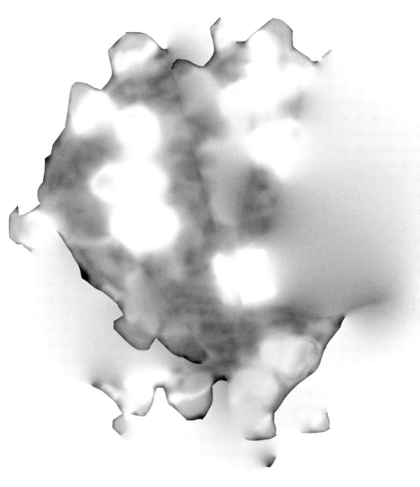

Hyperobjects are molten
and melting materialities,
nonlocal entities and
phased and interobjec-
tive things. As amalgams
of material, technological
and political entangle-
ments, they show the
new viscous condition
that postnatural ecologies
are facing.

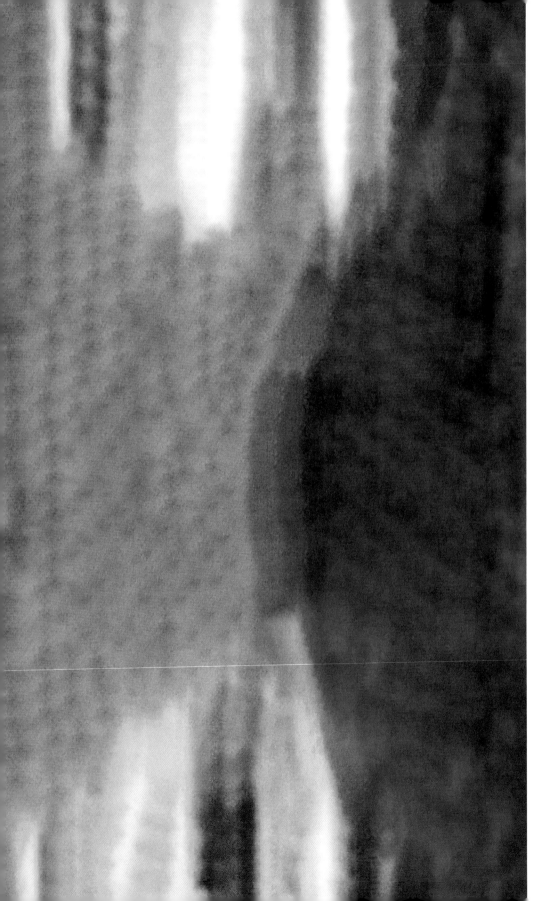

How can technology help the world share the feelings that are behind ecological issues and connect global problems with local manifestations? Can we propose other aesthetics that subvert the cleanliness and coldness of information related to the climate crisis? Should we propose a dark ecology of digital images that makes us rethink contemporary landscapes and definitely abandon a romanticized representation of nature?

Plastiglomerates are
postnatural stones
that contain mixtures
of sedimentary grains
and other natural
debris that are held
together by hardened
molten plastic. Another
potential marker of the
Anthropocene, they
become Melting Ecolo-
gies that defy scientists,
environmentalists and
geologists.

Speculative Ecologies:
The Future of Urban Wastelands

In conversation with Sandra Jasper, we delve into acoustic and cinematographic research methods to gain new perspectives on urban ecologies and to unpack more-than-human histories of so-called wastelands in Berlin.

JOHANNA JUST   In your work, you often discuss the sensorial qualities of urban space.[1] While you invite the reader to pay attention to more than visual effects in urban landscape design, you simultaneously focus on marginalized green spaces in the city. Can you describe your interest in these places (e.g. the Brachen of Berlin): What makes them important to study, or *to think with*, beyond their visual appearance? What does your focus on sensorial, acoustic qualities, allow you to unpack?

Interview with
Sandra Jasper

SANDRA JASPER   The visual representation of wastelands, and ruins especially, has a very long history. Often, these marginal spaces are romanticized, which can be problematic. Caitlin DeSilvey and Tim Edensor, for example, have written an insightful paper on the history of ruin scholarship entitled "Reckoning with Ruins."[2] They outline the shift from a Romantic conception of the ruin, and ruin-gazing as an aesthetic sensibility, to post-war engagements with traumatic memories evoked by ruins. They also highlight the persistency of ruin scholarship to privilege visual concerns and its preoccupation with 'the ruin' as a particular aesthetic or philosophical construct. In a way, this also applies to wastelands more generally. The focus of contemporary research on ruins is now shifting from preoccupations with post-industrial spaces to concerns with post-nuclear wasteland spaces and fast-paced extractive terrains that bear witness to devaluation or toxic legacies. Spaces of accelerating climatic volatility are already being abandoned and many places across the world are expected to become uninhabitable in the near future. Thus, ruins and wastelands proliferate and these spaces can be heavily stigmatized. But they may also be associated with future-bound possibilities of creativity and new beginnings.

1 Sandra Jasper, "Acoustic Botany: Listening to Nature in a Former Airfield," in *The Botanical City*, eds. Matthew Gandy and Sandra Jasper (Berlin: jovis, 2020), 221–28; Sandra Jasper, "Acoustic Ecologies: Architecture, Nature, and Modernist Experimentation in West Berlin," *Annals of the American Association of Geographers* 110, no. 4 (2020): 1114–33; Sandra Jasper, "Sonic Refugia: Nature, Noise Abatement and Landscape Design in West Berlin," *The Journal of Architecture* 23, no. 6 (2018): 936–60.

2 Caitlin DeSilvey and Tim Edensor, "Reckoning with Ruins," *Progress in Human Geography* 37, no. 4 (2013): 465–85.

3 Michael Gallagher, "Sounding Ruins: Reflections on the Production of an 'Audio Drift,'" *Cultural Geographies* 22, no. 3 (2015): 467–85; Ian Foreman, "Spectral Soundscapes: Exploring Spaces of Remembrance through Sound," *Interference: A Journal of Audio Culture* 4 (2014). Available from: interferencejournal.org/ spectral-soundscapes-exploring-spaces-of-remembrance-through-sound.

4 A. M. Kanngieser, "Sonic Colonialities: Listening, Dispossession, and the (re)Making of Anglo-European Nature," *Transactions of the Institute of British Geographers* (2023).

Researching wastelands in the field and being present there made me realize that the experience of wastelands is in fact multi-sensorial. What I have found interesting when conducting field research and also in the process of filmmaking is the acoustic dimension of these spaces. When walking through a city and entering a wasteland, the acoustics can change dramatically. The sound of traffic on busy roads tends to filter out other sounds such as those of birds, bees, insects, wind and human voices (that can be heard from a distance). To me, wastelands have an interesting acoustic character – they are messy: you might hear the sounds of cars and sirens in the distance, but you also may hear bees. Different scales and sounds blend together. I think what this does, as with other sensory experiences like haptic perception and sense of smell, is that it grounds the experience of a place in the human body.

What I also found revealing when researching wastelands was that sound can also produce distance. More researchers are now questioning the assumption that sound brings you closer to an environment. But sounds don't necessarily offer an immersive experience of a landscape or wasteland. Studies done by Michael Gallagher and Iain Foreman,[3] for instance, have looked into the soundscapes of ruins and abandoned spaces. They argue that absent sounds can create a distance, haunt or trigger certain memories. This work is also very interesting in relation to wastelands in terms of the forgotten or erased voices and histories of these spaces, which might be recovered through various sensory experiences.

JJ   Do you also take recordings yourself during your fieldwork?

SJ   Yes, I also work with field recording, but I am still learning. Doing field recording well is quite a complicated process. It is a delicate work: you really have to think about what you would like to record in urban environments. There are also important questions to be asked about the ethics and politics of producing, consuming and circulating sound recordings, even when we think about nonhuman sounds, as the geographer and sound artist A. M. Kanngieser has recently pointed out.[4] The practice of field recording has changed and diversified quite a bit since the 1930s. If we look at nature recordings, the practice has expanded from recording isolated single animal voices to so-called soundscape recordings. Field recording has been used as a method in bioacoustic research for the detection and identification of species, as well as to trace changes in animal communication and in soundscapes across time. But besides the field of bioacoustics, field recording has also been undertaken with more artistic approaches, for example by the World Soundscape Project in Vancouver in the 1960s and by CRESSON in Grenoble in the 1970s – two groups that focused on urban contexts.

SARA FRIKECH   Did you also learn how to interpret sound recordings?
Are there specific steps that you follow?

SJ   Yes. For me, this is a methodology that is moving and evolving.
There is also some literature discussing how to do this as well, as a longer
tradition around how to teach people how to listen.[5] This is something
I am drawing on from the wider context of sonic ecology. There are
methods that have been developed around listening on sound walks, for
example, and other forms of listening. There are also geographers doing
great work on listening including Jonathan Prior at Cardiff University and
A. M. Kanngieser based at Royal Holloway in London. And then there is
emerging literature on how to work with sound recordings. I think there
is less published around how to do this in an educational context or on
how to teach sound recording compared to filmmaking, which is maybe a
bigger field. So a lot of the work that I rely on comes from the arts, from
composers, sound recorders or artists working with these methodologies.
The artist and researcher Mark Peter Wright has just written a great book
Listening After Nature about the practice, theory and methodology of field
recording.[6]

SF   Moving towards filmmaking as research practice: in 2020 you
co-produced a documentary entirely devoted to the Brachen of Berlin.
How did *Natura Urbana* contribute to a different understanding of
so-called wastelands? What did cinematic research in this context allow
you to explore, which could not have been addressed in academic
writing? How did it help to construct a different perspective and –
being a highly seductive medium – how did it allow to bring marginalized urban green spaces into view and address questions surrounding
aesthetics? Did you encounter any ethical problems related to this?

SJ   I think there are many differences between academic writing and
filmmaking. Film communicates through an audio-visual language,
through moving images and sounds and also through rhythm and
temporality. It can evoke emotional responses. People are triggered
by certain scenes, which can bring back memories; you can't really
predetermine or anticipate these responses. With academic writing, this
is not the same – the kind of emotional response to an academic paper
would perhaps be a different one. In film, you don't have the possibility
of adding footnotes, where you contextualize, relativize and explain in
much more detail what your intentions were with a particular sentence
or, in the case of a film, with a particular scene. So you have to be quite
rigorous when you edit; editing is a huge part of filmmaking. Although a
documentary film might appear factual, it is in fact a highly constructed
medium. You can change the meaning of what you intend to say by
changing sequences or changing rhythms. Cutting an interview a bit
too early, or a bit too late, might change the meaning that is conveyed.

5 See, for example, Michael Gallagher, "Field Recording and the Sounding of Spaces," *Environment and Planning D: Society and Space* 33, no. 3 (2015): 560–76; Michael Gallagher, A. M. Kanngieser and Jonathan Prior, "Listening Geographies: Landscape, Affect and Geotechnologies," *Progress in Human Geography* 41, no. 5 (2017): 618–37; and Michel Chion, *Audio-Vision: Sound on Screen* (New York: Columbia University Press, 1990).

6 Mark Peter Wright, *Listening After Nature: Field Recording, Ecology, Critical Practice* (London: Bloomsbury, 2022).

With certain topics, what you are telling is quite delicate, so you have to be very careful in editing. What film also does is that it allows you to represent cities or wastelands or whatever the topic is through different angles, different scales, different perspectives or voices. You can include close-ups, far away angles – that's a very powerful tool. You can show different temporalities by including archival material or elicit future scenarios by including shots of cranes in the distance. In the case of filming wastelands, it was an important element to question the future of the places we studied.

Working with images and sounds together is very interesting as well. We worked with a great team: a very good sound recordist and designer Jonathan Schorr and editor Wiebke Hofmann. We gave Jonathan a lot of time to compose a layering of the soundscape using the field recordings that reflected what we wanted to say about wastelands.

Lastly, the film itself also becomes part of an archive because wastelands are such dynamic spaces and, in the case of Berlin, they are disappearing at a rapid pace. Similar to writing, film has the ability to document and capture a moment in time of a city. Perhaps fifty years from now the film might be used to revisit Berlin.

JJ   I really like that your academic work feeds into a cinematic piece and that in turn the film becomes an archive that can influence future academic work.

SJ   Yeah, film is a really good tool for academic work to reach out. I don't want to say that academic books do not reach a wide audience – they do. Maybe very specialized academic papers do less so. But I think the potential of filmmaking to reach really wide audiences is fantastic. As a piece in and of itself, but also as an educational tool: through screenings with students at different events or contexts, you reach diverse audiences. And you get many different responses. I think that this is sometimes what is meant by the idea of impact or science communication. I think there is a high potential for film to achieve this.

SF   Coming back to the question of editing: in filmmaking, you gather a lot of data, but then at one point, you have to be selective and decide what you show and what you don't show. How do you deal with that as a researcher?

SJ   I think this question touches on another important point: film is a collaborative project. Academic research is also a collaborative project, but in many cases, it is also an individual project. In the case of film, you really rely on specialists to help – at least in our project, we did. And deciding on the material to use was also a collaborative endeavour: it was a process whereby Matthew Gandy, the director,

Wiebke Hofmann, the editor and I were sitting together in the editing room, playing different scenes and experimenting with different selections of materials that we had filmed. And it was also a long process of discussion: What does the scene do? What is its role? The film, in a way, had its own trajectory; sometimes what we would have liked to communicate might not have been the same as what was necessary for the film at that point (i.e. what was required for people to understand what would follow).

We worked on this for a very long time; I think we spent eighteen months editing the film. And we had to say goodbye to some scenes that we really liked but that didn't make sense in the narrative of the film.

JJ   It seems that making a film is a time-consuming endeavour that differs greatly from the process of working on academic publications. How did filmmaking as a research method impact you as an academic? What did it enable and how did it restrict you?

SJ   First of all, to work on a documentary – on something that is so different – was a fantastic opportunity after completing my PhD. I am really grateful to Matthew Gandy and the ERC project for bringing me into the project. It was a different working experience from writing up my thesis, where I was sitting alone at my desk; it was a very nice change. But it was also quite a risky thing to do. Because if you look at an academic career, the postdoctoral phase is the moment – especially in the current context of academic job markets – defining what makes or breaks you, whether you enter academia and have a career or not. It is a very difficult moment. And it is not always clear whether working on a documentary film will be recognized as proper scientific work. So we are still in the process of acknowledging that and having it be more accepted. A documentary is certainly valued differently compared to scientific publications when it comes to ranking academics and their achievements – which we have to be critical of. So it was a risky endeavour in that sense.

As an academic, filmmaking has impacted me in many different ways. First of all, it allowed me to see that what I had researched previously (as part of my PhD) could be built into a film: I worked on the cultural and environmental history of West Berlin and some of the chapters in the film connected to my thesis. So it was exciting to look at some of the archival materials again and try to build these materials into the narrative of the film. Learning how to make a film on the ERC project also enabled me to continue on with this work. I train students in seminars on filmmaking, and some of my students now finish their Master's degrees with documentary films. And I also continue to work with sound and field recording. So, filmmaking enabled a lot for me, but it also restricted me timewise. You could say that I have a 'publication gap' during the time I worked on *Natura Urbana*.

SF   Do you see a potential for filmmaking to become part of a wider methodology in urban and landscape studies? If so, could it become more embedded in academia as a methodology that allows challenging cinematic formats and contributes to knowledge production in academia?

SJ   I think documentary filmmaking is already a methodology that has a history in urban and landscape studies. It is maybe not part of current curricula in these disciplines. But when you think about geography, and the history of explorers, they were using different kinds of methods, including at some point also film – often documentary footage, now perhaps buried in archives. I think there is a long history of using these kinds of methods that we need to revisit. And we need to start thinking about the ethics and politics of using documentary film and sound recording as methods in our own research projects. In terms of training students, it is important to not only teach how to critically engage with representations that already exist but also to teach how to make them – how to *make* representations through sound recording and film – and what this means. I think this part is still missing somehow in our current curricula.

Then, there's also film as a different type of methodology. If, for example, you use video recordings for interviews and then interpret that material, that might be different from making a film, which in and of itself becomes the final output of a research project. So there are numerous ways of engaging with film in geography, urban studies or landscape research – interpreting existing films, using filmmaking as a methodology and making a film as a research project. I think what *critical* documentary filmmaking can also do is challenge other existing films. There are a lot of problematic narratives and representations in existing films that we might challenge not only through writing but also through filmmaking.

JJ   I wanted to follow up on the question of ethics when working on documentary films. How does the medium of film in contrast to academic publishing change the way you construct an argument using interviews or recordings?

SJ   This is an important question. For example, with some of the protagonists that feature in *Natura Urbana*, we also had a back and forth – as you are also supposed to do with papers – giving them transcripts and asking them if they were ok with the scene, having them involved in this decision. Some film interviews were like an hour long. And in the end, in the editing process, we chose a few seconds of the interview and then we even chose a few seconds of a different scene and cut them together. This is a radical thing to do, especially if you interview academics who are so careful about what they say.

So that was important. It was also important that Matthew and I knew the people featured in the film; Matthew had worked with some of the academics before. So there was a shared level of trust in making the film and cutting everything together. And it was really important to have that trust. We also had one person who came into the film by chance, the community activist who appeared towards the end of the film, who was just present and was eager to say something. She had some great points to make about gentrification, landscaping and the politics around urban change. Then there are many ethical things to consider when putting people next to each other – people who are very eloquent next to people who are maybe not that eloquent, or less familiar with academic terms, etc. We had many discussions about how to make people appear in the best way – it was quite complicated in that sense.

ᴊᴊ Do you continue working with filmmaking and other sensorial methodologies in your research and are you interested in exploring these methodologies further?

 sᴊ I am still involved in filmmaking, currently mostly through teaching. Along with my colleagues Laura Kemmer and Sylvana Jahre, I have been teaching Master's students how to create films for their final projects. Together with Nitin Bathla, Falma Fshazi, Henrik Ernstson, Sofie Stilling, Klearjos Papanicolaou and other people who are part of an emerging film and urban research network, I am establishing a platform for academics, filmmakers, producers, doctoral students and other people working across the worlds of academia and filmmaking. I have also just started a new sound research project together with the geographer Jonathan Prior. In this project, 'Listening to the Archive,' which is funded by the Leverhulme Trust, we critically engage with the history of animal sound recordings and their collection in the two largest wildlife sound archives in Europe: The British Library's Wildlife and Environmental Sounds collection and the Animal Sound Archive at the Museum für Naturkunde Berlin. In the future, we also hope to collaborate with field recordists, researching their collections, and to develop creative audio formats as part of our research. So that would be the next project. •

A Berlin Ostkreuz
wasteland. Former
wasteland at
Glasbläserallee, Berlin.
Photograph. Sandra
Jasper, 2015.

Interview with
Sandra Jasper

B Berlin Pankow railway wasteland. The 34-hectare railway wasteland in Pankow harbours the last natterjack toads in Berlin. Photograph. Sandra Jasper, 2020.

C Berlin Südgelände Nature Park. Natur-Park Südgelände, Berlin. Biodiverse meadows in a former railway wasteland. Photograph. Sandra Jasper, 2015.

D Berlin Wilmersdorf interstitial space. Wild flower meadow on a boulevard, Berlin. Photograph. Sandra Jasper, 2020.

E Berlin Südgelände Nature Park. Natur-Park Südgelände, Berlin. Biodiverse meadows in a former railway wasteland. Photograph. Sandra Jasper, 2015.

The Trap of Time: Prototyping a Summer School

Federico Pérez Villoro tests alternate curricula with Materia Abierta, a summer school in Mexico City, reiterating learning models and offering a space to reflect on the ethics of the present and the future.

PROTOTYPING

ITERATIONS

DESIGN PROTOTYPE MODEL FINAL VERSION DISTRIBUTION

TESTS REPRODUCIBILITY

Federico
Pérez Villoro

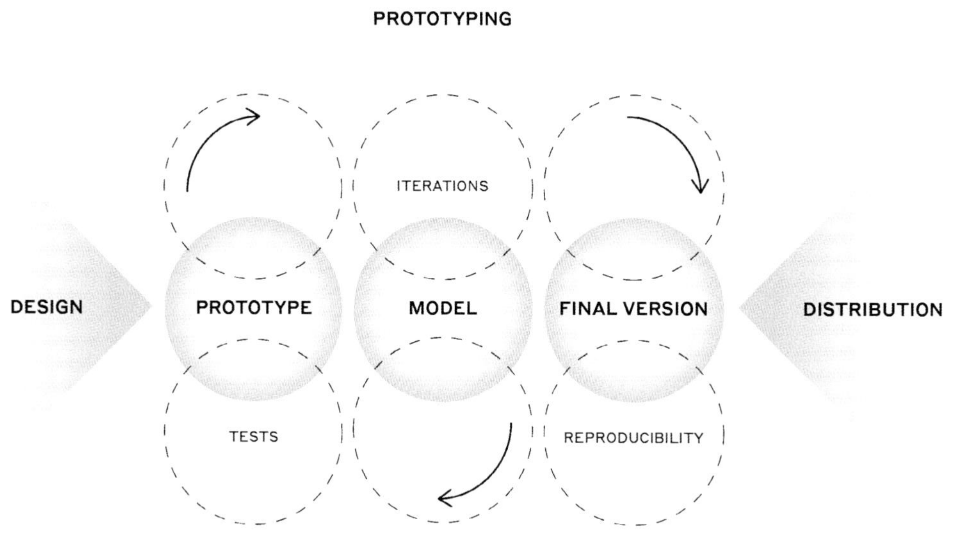

Materia Abierta is a summer school on theory, art and technology established in Mexico City. Conceived as a space to reflect on the urgency of our presents and futures, the programme aims to interrogate the political, economic and ideological forces that condition contemporary cultural production today and to favour other forms of action and knowledge. Under the premise of being a permanent prototype of itself, it is reconfigured each year exercising evolving educational models. This text elaborates on Materia Abierta's prototype metaphor and considers its possible inadequacy, given that it is inevitably linked to a linear construction of time that the programme rejects and to the promise of an ultimate version that in this case will never come. Prototypes are temporary representations of products or services that are to be improved. They serve as provisional evidence to justify designs and anticipate shortcomings. In addition, they demonstrate their replicable condition: they contain encoded patterns that make them reproducible. When we say that Materia Abierta is a prototype of itself,

66

1 "I'll be your interface," at the Welcome to Tomorrow, Today workshop held by Second Thoughts (co-founders of Materia Abierta), Mexico City, November 13–14, 2015.

however, the emphasis is on its incomplete, indeterminate, imperfect state. It is the rejection of a suitable format and of any repeatable formula. We seek for each iteration to be exposed to unexpected conditions in order to open deep rearrangements in our learning ritual.

During a workshop we organized in 2015, in an exercise prior to Materia Abierta, designer David Reinfurt refers to J. G. Ballard's idea of science fiction perhaps being "the best sort of realism. Maybe the only possible one."[1] This idea gave participants a point of departure to think about the future as a better guide for the present than the past. However, in recent years the space for speculation has narrowed. It is increasingly difficult to imagine societies in distant futures; the worlds that we can envision, closer in time, are dramatically different from those that we have taken for granted.

Discussing the future, then, requires recognizing it as a rhetorical construction in the function of capital and its various forms of oppression. This was the starting point of Materia Abierta's 2021 edition. In the words of Mônica Hoff and Eva Posas, the curators of the programme, "As a project of condemnation or salvation, the idea of the future is intertwined with linearity of time defined by epistemologies and colonial narratives of conquest, dispossession and domination. Therefore, the concepts created to name it are not only endless but insufficient, given that beyond the end of the future as the end of the world, what we are really facing is the exhaustion of a civilizing project built in the order of reason."[2]

Studying the future can be paradoxical. On the one hand, it can be an excuse to disengage with the past; on the other, it is imperative to find ways out of the contemporary neo-liberal economic paradigm. How can we approach current problems with the urgency they demand without reproducing the conceptual trap of time?

Our 2021 programme aimed to disarm both the messianic myth of a better future and the (increasingly accepted and comfortable) apocalyptic imaginary of the hereafter. The future in Edenic terms operates under the common pretext that the salvation of humanity is arranged in an expression of itself that is not yet present. Thus, the dismissing of current collective action and the projection of civic responsibility towards the future obfuscates versions of the present that have already manifested themselves and that demonstrate feasible and more just social expressions than their dominant counterparts.

"We have to put the past in front of us," said philosopher Luciana Parisi during a seminar she gave as part of our programme.[3] It was an invitation to rethink the spacetime geometries that support the illusion that the apocalypse is yet to happen. Her article "Recursive Colonialism and Cosmo-Computation," co-authored with Ezekiel Dixon-Román, addresses how the threat of the end of the world justifies social exploitation under the promise of interrupting the self-destruction of the Western white subject.[4] In anticipation of its own limits, the technoscientific model reproduces its inherent violence. Parisi and Dixon-Román argue that colonialism is reformulated by integrating unexpected events over time – domination is updated recursively through processes of self-adaptation, self-regulation and self-regeneration.

The risk of the unknown cyclically imposes the rationalist order. In the words of Parisi and Dixon-Román: "The monologic universalism in the epistemic response to the emergence of contingency creates the apocalyptic scenario where the end of capital is also the end of the human and of freedom."[5] This inevitably reminds us of the phrase that is repeated like a mantra in academic contexts that study the future and whose authorship has been blurred: "It is easier to imagine the end of the world than the end of capitalism." A statement that certainly has its place, but is

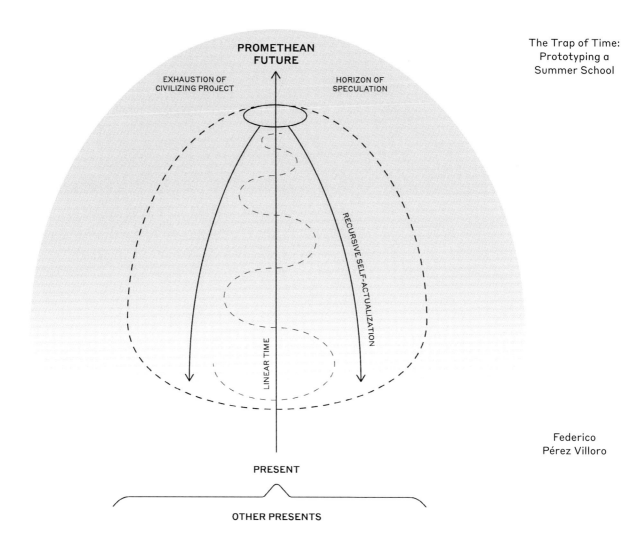

PROMETHEAN
FUTURE

EXHAUSTION OF
CIVILIZING PROJECT

HORIZON OF
SPECULATION

RECURSIVE SELF-ACTUALIZATION

LINEAR TIME

PRESENT

OTHER PRESENTS

Federico
Pérez Villoro

also incomplete: What version of the world does this end of the world refer to?

Recursivity is the capacity through which a process establishes itself based on its own definition. Recursive systems are capable of assigning their organization from a constant negotiation between structure and function. It is a common feature of contemporary computing. Layers within neural networks move data in a cyclical way while dividing it into multiple versions of itself seeking to self-evaluate the efficiency of its results. As information flows, the network incorporates the processing experience and modifies its programmatic nodes in a continuous exercise of abstraction and comparison.

This level of calculus is closer to simulation than prototyping: it depends on the experimental processing of information to evaluate functions under sets of criteria over time. As writer Nora N. Khan points out, simulations are "both literal products of equations that describe what actions can happen inside of a virtual world, and potent metaphors for future-casting."[6] They are processes that execute

68

2 Mônica Hoff and Eva Posas, "Ni apocalipsis ni paraíso: Meditaciones en el umbral," Summer programme curatorial summary, August 17 – September 18, 2021. 2021.materiaabierta.com.

3 Seminar held by Luciana Parisi at Materia Abierta, Mexico City, September 10, 2021. 2021.materiaabierta.com.

4 Luciana Parisi and Ezekiel Dixon-Román, "Recursive Colonialism and Cosmo-Computation," *Social Text* (2020). socialtextjournal.org/ periscope_article/ recursive-colonialism-and-cosmo-computation.

5 Parisi and Dixon-Román, "Recursive Colonialism."

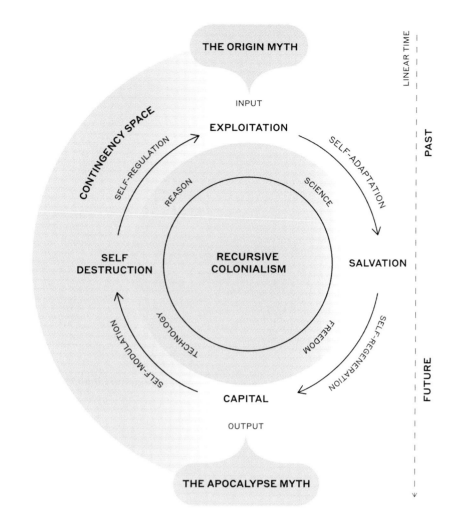

"hypothetical scenarios" through different conditions, capturing the behaviour of a model in full action.

Simulations allow us to imagine situations that are not yet available by means through which we base our actions. As we learned from Patricia Reed during a seminar that we organized with her in the summer of 2020: "The human capacity to conceptually unbind thought from the present (in both space and time) is where the relationship between care and risk can be articulated as a crucial dynamic for thinking planetary-dimensioned social worlds."[7] But how can we make those worlds of the 'there and then' intelligible in the 'here and now'? Is it possible to reorient the metric of time through the predictive logic of algorithms?

These questions resonate with the initial edition of Materia Abierta in 2019. That edition addressed how, although the current power of computers allows the construction and distribution of innumerable simulations that are convenient for perceiving the world, these programmes respond to their own training logic. In the words of its curator

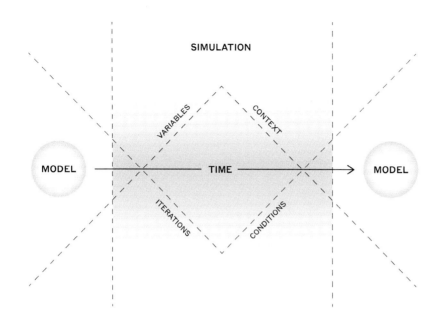

Federico
Pérez Villoro

Natalia Zuluaga: "The tightening feedback loop between media, knowledge, lived experience and the environment is not merely a concern for today. The future is trapped in an endless financialized exchange with the present; a loop that all but guarantees that the inequality, detention and violence enacted upon racialized and marginalized bodies will endure."[8]

Parisi's work, however, insists on the possibility of critical computation to generate epistemologies that go beyond universal techno-scientific certainties. Specifically,

she refers to the abductive logic of algorithms as a reason space that distinguishes itself from data analysis by generating new forms of logical complexity outside the "statistical regime of inductive capital." This generates what Parisi calls, in reference to the ideas of Charles Sanders Peirce, a "meta-hypothetical" function capable of inferring speculative hypotheses about unknown phenomena. In other words, abductive automation offers explanations beyond a "linear sequence of given causes and effects."[9]

Unlike the conventional prototype, the

70

6 Nora N. Khan, "Seeing, Naming, Knowing," *The Brooklyn Rail*, March 2019. brooklynrail. org/2019/03/art/ seeing-naming-knowing.

7 Patricia Reed, "Sobre mundos habitables y planetarios," in the Futuros posibles programme hosted by Materia Abierta, Casa del Lago UNAM and Museo Tamayo, Seminar August 11, 13 and 15, 2020. museotamayo. org/futuros-posibles-2/ patricia-reed.

8 Natalia Zuluaga, inaugural edition Materia Abierta, August 5–6, 2019. materiaabierta.com.

9 Luciana Parisi, "Critical Computation: Digital Automata and General Artificial Thinking," *Theory, Culture & Society* 36, no. 2 (2019): 89–121.

10 Parisi, "Critical Computation" (see note 9).

11 Luciana Parisi and Ezekiel Dixon-Román, "Data Capitalism, Sociogenic Prediction, and Recursive Indeterminacies," in *Data Publics* (Milton Park, Abingdon, Oxon; New York, NY: Routledge, 2020), 48–62.

12 Parisi and Dixon-Román, "Data Capitalism" (see note 11).

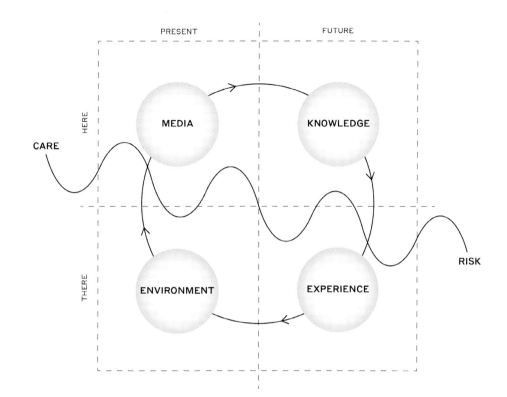

recursive model is not a static representation of material possibilities. It is, moreover, incomplete in the first instance: in its abduction potential, it sustains a permanent disposition to change and has built within its internal logics a self-transforming factor that is beyond the characteristics from which it is designed. In fact, its operational rules arise from the automatic behaviour of the data. As Parisi points out, "machine learning is the inverse of programming: the question is not to deduce the output from a given algorithm, but rather to find the algorithm that produces this output."[10]

The recursive temporality of computational systems reveals their incomplete state and therefore the systemic impossibility of modern techno-epistemic principles. In this sense, Parisi and Dixon-Román suggest that current computing not only reflects the normativity of knowledge production but also that by including indeterminate elements, the Promethean progress of recursive colonialism is weakened.[11] However, the rejection of a universal technological programme would require that algorithms take advantage of the gaps

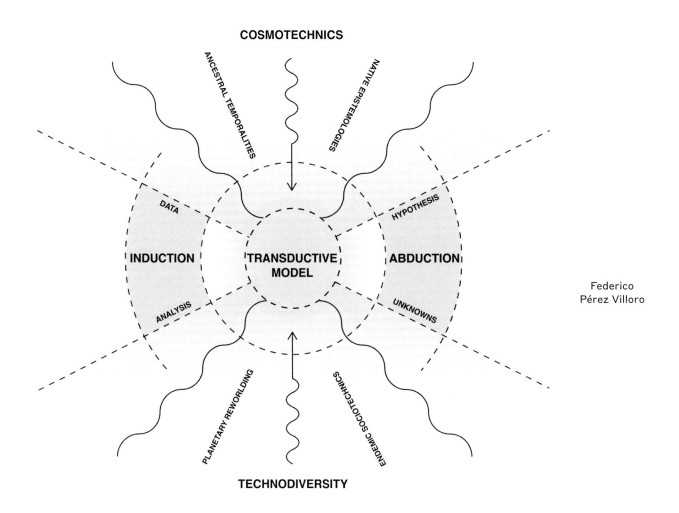

Federico
Pérez Villoro

caused by recursion to become infected with a multiplicity of localized transversal cosmologies, which philosopher Yuk Hui calls cosmotechnics.

Predictive algorithms do not only work from retroactive analysis of existing data but instead incorporate incomplete information as part of their own learning process. In the words of Parisi and Dixon-Román: "The interaction between data sets, contexts, and algorithmic rules entails not a recursive learning, but a trans-ductive learning."[12] It is in this sense that the deviation from the linear progress of modern knowledge requires a transformation of the technical systems from which knowledge is generated so that they include indeterminate possibilities at all their procedural levels.

The trans-ductive potential of these systems can serve as an unfinished, imprecise, indefinitely adaptable guide for our pedagogical project. However, when considering this, it is crucial to not lose sight of the way in which colonial capital evolves in conjunction with machines and with epistemological narratives around them. How to imagine, then, a learning model beyond the limits of reason? How to avoid reproducing the excluding logics of the institutionalization of knowledge? How to escape from cognitive capitalism? How to stop specifying the world under temporal metrics of empire? Is the recovery of critique outside of an epistemic quest? Do acts of refusal need to be symbolically represented? How to destabilize the aesthetic relationship between the future and technology? How can we avoid reproducing extractivist logics in our theorization?

At a time when education is rapidly being rearranged, the value of educational institutions is being put to the test. The cost of keeping schools running is at odds with their concrete offerings, and the move to educate online exposes the institutional structures that seem better suited to protect academic markets than student needs. This is not just one more effect of the pandemic but of the progressive crisis of the privatization of knowledge and the procurement of false meritocratic systems. But what are the essential components of schools and what are their administrative surpluses? Is it possible to reimagine online learning and make our programmes more accessible? How to take advantage of virtual spaces while considering the mechanisms that benefit from digital overproductivity?

Materia Abierta is a small effort to address the need to develop new learning space as profound recalibrations of educational logics. As an epistemic and political space, the programme seeks to weave links between the worlds that have been made evident and those that are less visible or have been historically obscured. It is a call to ritualize critical socialization, awaken collective imagination and conjure up insurrectionary imaginaries in search of shared realities beyond the versions of the future from which it is necessary to escape. •

Federico
Pérez Villoro

A C
D
B E

A Public Lecture by Yásnaya Elena Aguilar Gil during Materia Abierta's 2019 programme.

B Visit to El Cerro Gordo in Ecaptepec, Mexico City with members of MACE (Museo Arte Contemporáneo Ecatepec).

C Performance resulting from Vaginal Davis's workshop during Materia Abierta's 2019 programme.

D Still from Maximiliano Mamani's performance "El orden de las rosas," commissioned as part of Materia Abierta's 2021 programme.

E Materia Abierta's participants at Calpulli Tecalco in San Pedro Atocpan, Milpa Alta.

Contributors

LUIZA PRADO DE O. MARTINS is an artist, writer and researcher whose work examines themes of reproduction, herbal medicine, coloniality, gender and race. She is part of the curatorial board of transmediale 2021 and an assistant professor and vice-director of the Centre for Other Worlds at the Lusófona University in Lisbon. She is a founding member of Decolonising Design. Her ongoing artistic research project, 'A Topography of Excesses,' looks into encounters between human and plant beings within the context of herbalist reproductive medicine, approaching these practices as expressions of radical care.

CHRISTINA GRUBER is a Vienna-based freshwater ecologist, visual artist and sturgeon caretaker. Water is of special interest to her as it is the connector between stories of different places and layers, from clouds to data centres. In the last years, she has navigated large rivers (from the Mississippi to the Danube), exploring interspecies relationships, alternative forms of care, political resilience and ecological pedagogy using speculative narration. She currently teaches at the University of Applied Arts Vienna, the University of Art and Design Linz and is engaged in artistic research projects dealing with acoustic ecology along rivers.

KARIN REISINGER holds a PhD in Visual Culture and is an architect. She is currently a research fellow of the Austrian Science Fund (FWF) Hertha Firnberg Fellowship at the Institute for Education in the Arts, Academy of Fine Arts Vienna, where she also teaches and leads the FWF project 'Stories of Post-extractive Feminist Futures.' Previous fellowships include research at KTH Stockholm School of Architecture, where she engaged with the mining areas of Sápmi / northern Sweden and at ArkDes Stockholm, where she critically examined the architectural archives on exploited peripheries. Reisinger focuses on marginalized perspectives from mining landscapes through participatory lectures, contributions to archives, walking seminars and writings; she recently curated 'Fences Insects Embroideries (material communities)' as part of Wienwoche 2022.

DELUS

THE INSTITUTE FOR POSTNATURAL STUDIES is a centre for artistic experimentation from which to explore and problematize post-nature as a framework for contemporary creation. Founded in 2020, it is conceived as a platform for critical thinking, a network that brings together artists and researchers concerned about the issues of the global ecological crisis through experimental formats of exchange and the production of open knowledge. From a multidisciplinary approach, the Institute develops long-term research focused on issues such as ecology, coexistence, politics and territories. These lines of investigation take different shapes and formats, including seminars, exhibitions and residencies as spaces for academic and artistic experimentation.

SANDRA JASPER is Assistant Professor for Geography of Gender in Human-Environment-Systems at the Humboldt-Universität of Berlin. Her research interests are in urban nature, soundscapes and feminist theory. She is co-editor (with Matthew Gandy) of *The Botanical City* (JOVIS, 2020)

and is currently completing a monograph on the experimental spaces of West Berlin for which she received a Graham Foundation grant. Her research has been published among other journals in the *Annals of the American Association of Geographers, The Journal of Architecture* and *Dialogues in Human Geography*.

FEDERICO PÉREZ VILLORO is an artist and researcher living and working in Mexico City. Through texts, performances and digital artefacts, Pérez Villoro explores the ways in which state, corporate and institutional authority is exercised technologically. His work has been exhibited internationally and published by *The Serving Library*, Printed Matter, *C Magazine, diSONARE, Gato Negro* and the Walker Art Center's *The Gradient*. Pérez Villoro has taught at the Rhode Island School of Design and California College of the Arts and lectured at schools such as ETH Zürich, Rutgers University, CalArts, The New School, UNAM and Hongik University. He recently founded Materia Abierta, a summer school on theory, art and technology based in Mexico City.

DELUS
The Journal of the Institute of Landscape and Urban Studies

Issue 0
Autumn 2023

DELUS is an annual, interdisciplinary publication by the Institute of Landscape and Urban Studies, ETH Zürich.

FOUNDING EDITORS
Sara Frikech and Johanna Just

PROJECT MANAGEMENT
Dorothee Hahn

COPYEDITING
Liana Simmons

PROOFREADING
Irene Schaudies

GRAPHIC DESIGN
Studio Folder

PRODUCTION
Alise Ausmane, Hatje Cantz

REPRODUCTIONS
ReproMayer Medienproduktion GmbH, Reutlingen

PRINTING AND BINDING
Livonia Print, Riga

PAPER
Magno Volume, 150 g/m²

TYPOGRAPHY
Styrene B (Berton Hasebe and Ilya Ruderman, 2016)
Louize (Matthieu Cortat, 2011)

In its commitment to adhere to copyright regulations, DELUS Journal has diligently strived to ensure compliance. The images presented in this publication are either cleared of copyright restrictions, published in alignment with the Creative Commons (CC) licensing terms or have been incorporated with explicit written permission from the respective copyright holders. However, if you are a copyright owner and harbour concerns regarding potential infringements, we kindly request that you reach out to the editors.

PUBLISHED BY
Hatje Cantz Verlag GmbH
Mommsenstraße 27
10629 Berlin
www.hatjecantz.de
A Ganske Publishing Group Company

ISBN 978-3-7757-5636-5
ISBN ePDF 978-3-7757-5637-2
ISSN 2941-6515
ISSN online 2941-6531

Printed in Latvia.

Significant support is provided by the Institute of Landscape and Urban Studies, ETH Zürich. A debt of gratitude is owed to Teresa Galí-Izard and Freek Persyn for their generous support and trust in DELUS.

THANKS
Tom Avermaete
Nitin Bathla
Joël Berger
Seppe De Blust
Maria Conen
Jennifer Duyne Barenstein
Moritz Gleich
Nicole la Hausse de Lalouvière
Michiel van Iersel
Ina Valkanova
Hubert Klumpner
Sabine Sarwa
Milica Topalović
Nazlı Tümerdem

DELUS

COVER IMAGE
A Russian sturgeon (*Acipenser gueldenstaedtii*) from the hatchery on the Danube Island. Photograph. Christina Gruber, 2020.